W9-CNY-466

A Providential Anti-Semitism

Nationalism and Polity in Nineteenth Century Romania

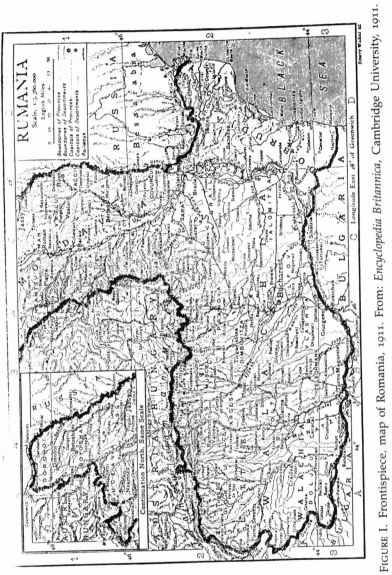

FIGURE I. Frontispiece, map of Romania, 1911. From: *Encyclopedia Britannica*, Cambridge University, 1911.

A Providential Anti-Semitism

Nationalism and Polity in Nineteenth Century Romania

WILLIAM O. OLDSON

THE AMERICAN PHILOSOPHICAL SOCIETY

INDEPENDENCE SQUARE: PHILADELPHIA

MEMOIRS OF THE
AMERICAN PHILOSOPHICAL SOCIETY
HELD AT PHILADELPHIA
FOR PROMOTING USEFUL KNOWLEDGE
VOLUME 193

Cover design by Fran Schultzberg. The Lion of Judah is shown against the colors of the Romanian flag.

This book was subsidized in part by the John Frederick Lewis Award of the American Philosophical Society.

Library of Congress Catalog Card Number: 90-56109
International Standard Book Number 0-87169-193-0
US ISSN: 0065-9738

For

Judy, Darren, and Scott

Contents

Illustrations

Preface

In order to assist those who might wish to peruse the materials used to research this study, I have retained the orthography and spellings of the Romanian originals. The reader, then, will discover in the footnotes and bibliography some considerable variance in the rendering of Romanian words and, on occasion, of proper names. Except for the spelling of the country's name (i.e., "România" in the native language, "Roumanie" and "Rumänien" in the French and German versions respectively, and their Anglicized forms), few such variations appear in the body of the text.

Though I am solely responsible for the analysis and judgments contained herein on the sui generis nature of Romanian anti-Semitism, I do owe a considerable debt to my colleagues and friends who have commented on the manuscript. I very much appreciate the historical expertise and sensitivity displayed in assisting me in avoiding the all too obvious perils present in discussing a variant form of anti-Semitism. They helped me present more compellingly an extraordinary bias which could rationalize brutalizing this segment of Romania's population and at the same time refuse to cooperate fully with the Nazis' extermination program. I want to express a special sense of gratitude to Neil Betten, Mark Goldman, and Rabbi Joseph Levenson for the thoroughness with which they read the manuscript. Their observations, as well as the kindness with which these were offered, provided me with the insights required to document more accurately the ideological background for the Balkan chapter of the Holocaust.

Tallahassee, May 1989   W. O. O.

Introduction

An oxymoron when encountered in literature usually startles us, compelling a broadening of our appreciation for the connotative value of certain words. Perhaps, after such a jolt, we even rethink the concepts they represent. It does not lessen the force or content of either. The title of this volume is a good example — the idea of "providence" would appear to be incongruously placed along side that of extraordinary prejudice directed against the Jewish community. We need an expanded model for anti-Semitism, however, in order to explain in both theory and practice the peculiarities of Romanian ethnic partisanship. For the traditional explanations of anti-Semitism, at least as applied to the more familiar areas of Europe, simply do not allow for what occurred in Romania during World War II. This oxymoron then may force us to look once more, with increased attention and without the blinkers of accustomed notions, at the nature and impact of bias. In the Romanian context it will certainly oblige us to define more accurately anti-Semitism's interaction with romantic nationalism. Obviously no attempt is being made to explain away the horrors of the Holocaust in Romania nor to indicate that such an obscenity can be tolerated by civilized peoples. Unless we expand our perception of prejudice and how that complex of emotion laden concepts can be expressed, however, we will be left with an incomplete, shallow understanding of one of the most unusual experiences of the Jewish community during the Nazi era; namely, the survival of hundreds of thousands of Romanian Jews in an anti-Semitic society which had the worst reputation in Europe for brutality. Through the fortuities of geography and the mental cast of the anti-Semitic Romanian intelligentsia, this largest of the Jewish communities in the Balkans survived. The "providential" quality of this anti-Semitism rested on the nationalistic self-interest of the Romanians rather than on any benevolence or the absence of aggression towards Jews. At least in this limited sense it did constitute a providential occurrence. Without it the Romanian Jewish community would likely have experienced the more thoroughgoing portion of most other East European Jews.

Hannah Arendt, herself a refugee from the persecutions of Nazi Germany and a most thoughtful analyst concerning the characteristics of dictatorship and anti-Semitism, labeled Romania "the most anti-Semitic country in prewar Europe . . . where even the S.S. were taken aback, and occasionally frightened, by the horrors of old-fashioned, spontaneous pogroms on a gigantic scale. . . ."[1] Certainly in terms of the savagery demonstrated by the Romanians during World War II, she cannot be accused of exaggeration. Contemporary accounts of what the Iron Guard did to the Jewish community of Bucharest[2] or of the actions taken by the Romanian army in Bessarabia and Bucovina in executing Marshal Ion Antonescu's version of the "Final Solution"[3] approach the unreadable. In Iași, the Moldavian capital and focal point of the most virulent Romanian anti-Semitism, the massacres of Jews during the wartime period beggar the imagination. Whether we read summaries in secondary works[4] or brief eyewitness descriptions detailing how the atrocities proceeded, we will be nauseated.[5] Finally, the thoroughness along with the exceptional cruelty exhibited made Romanian anti-Semitism during the Second World War stand out even in the extraordinary spectrum of contemporary European authoritarian states. Romania under the Iron Guard and later Marshal Antonescu as *Con-*

[1] Hannah Arendt, *Eichmann in Jerusalem* (New York: Viking Press, 1963), 172.

[2] Emil Dorian, *The Quality of Witness, A Romanian Diary 1937–1944.* Trans. Mara Soceanu Vamos. (Philadelphia: The Jewish Publication Society of America, 1982), 137–9.

[3] Matatias Carp, *Cartea Neagra, Suferințele Evreilor din România, 1940–1944,* I–III, (Bucharest: 1946–48).

[4] Jean Ancel, "The Jassy Syndrome (I)," *Romanian Jewish Studies,* I(1987), nr. 1: 33–49; *idem,* "The Jassy Syndrome (II)," *Romanian Jewish Studies,* I(1987), nr. 2: 35–52.

[5] Nicholas M. Nagy-Talavera, *The Green Shirts and the Others, A History of Fascism in Hungary and Rumania* (Stanford: Hoover Institute Press, 1970), 333.

ducătorul ("The Leader") furnished irrefutable proof for Arendt's thesis on the brutish expression of its anti-Semitism. That state had the distinction of being second only to Nazi Germany in the completeness of its pursuit of the Jewish community from identification to inhumane transport to mass murder.[6] This dismal record is not improved upon nor is Romania's reputation as "the most anti-Semitic state" in Europe mitigated by the historiography of the Communist period. While acknowledging the attempted genocide directed against Romania's Jewish community, the approach has been to pursue exculpation by blurring the distinctions between the Iron Guard and Marshal Antonescu's fascist government. Such attempts at vindication also attribute any and all anti-Semitic outbursts to the baleful effects of bourgeois society.[7] Indeed, this type of history either overlooks entirely or downplays that element of anti-Semitism which has constituted one of the most enduring and ingrained aspects of Romanian nationalism. Despite a long history of disabilities[8] directed against its Jewish community and a determined effort to deny the rights of citizenship whenever possible, such studies gloss over widespread native participation. Or they attempt to explain away obvious manifestations of Romanian anti-Semitism. Behind a facade of historic analysis these nationalistic drills serve the function of directing the uninformed reader's attention elsewhere. Thus he would never guess that in the mid-nineteenth century and again after World War I the Western Powers had placed considerable pressure upon the Romanian state to remove the legal disabilities[9] encumbering that society's Jewish population.

---

[6] Dorian, *The Quality of Witness*, xxxi.

[7] Aurel Karețki & Maria Covaci, *Zile însângerate la Iași, (28–30 iunie 1941)* (București: Editura Politică, 1978), 15, 112–3.

[8] The traditional term "Jewish disabilities" summed up the hostile environment in Romania. Scholars employed it in discussing the legal as well as extra-legal restraints inflicted on the Jewish community. Since those not well read in the area of anti-Semitism might interpret this usage as indicating some purported deficiency on the part of the persecuted minority, in most instances it has been rendered as "anti-Jewish disabilities." Where Romanian society's repressive intent towards the Jewish population could not be missed and no misunderstanding seemed likely, the customary usage has been retained.

[9] As detailed in the 1872 petition of Romanian Jews to the country's legislature, these traditional anti-Jewish disabilities included more than deprivation of civil and political rights. Prohibitions against Jews owning or farming rural properties, purchasing their homes, entering the learned professions, or being promoted in the army (where they had to serve) aggravated the sense of being singled out for prejudicial

Unfortunately, these efforts usually remained futile. The disingenuousness remains such, though, that these tensions are simply omitted from consideration.[10]

The other half of the title's oxymoron comes into play at this point. Hannah Arendt's description of Romania as "the most anti-Semitic country in prewar Europe" though very apt leaves us puzzled in light of her later assertion regarding survival statistics. She observed that, "About half of Rumania's eight hundred and fifty thousand Jews survived, a great number of whom—several hundred thousand—found their way to Israel."[11] As a matter of fact the large Romania created at Versailles had in 1939 between 757,000 and 800,000 Jewish inhabitants constituting approximately 4.2 percent of the population. By the spring of 1945 that number had shrunk to 428,000–430,000 survivors. The vast majority of those murdered resided either in northwest Transylvania (given to Hungary in the Vienna Award of 30 August 1940) or in the northeast along the border with the Soviet Union (in Bessarabia and Bucovina, much of which is now in the Moldavian S.S.R.). Interestingly and of the greatest significance to the Romanian Jewish community's survival, those who lived through World War II came mainly from the Old Kingdom (that is, from within the pre-World War I borders of Romania).[12] As odd as it now seems, the Romanians carried out their pogroms in a selective fashion killing primarily "enemy" or "foreign" Jews. They did indeed butcher a majority of the Jewish community in Bessarabia and Bucovina, but they did not attack (or allow the Germans to take) the bulk of their "own" Jews. Granted that any violent expression of prejudice cannot be condoned, this still remains a delicacy of discrimination not to be expected. We would not look for such self-serving shrewdness in what has been labeled, quite correctly, "the most anti-Semitic country in prewar Europe." Such selectivity by various elements within

---

treatment. Such restrictions on the Jewish community were well established by the time the Congress of Berlin convened in 1878. See Max J. Kohler & Simon Wolf, *Jewish Disabilities in the Balkan States* (New York: The American Jewish Committee, 1916), 98–101.

[10] Karetki & Covaci, *Zile însângerate la Iași*, 18–9; see the bowdlerized "Introduction" as a whole for a typical example of such scholarship.

[11] Arendt, *Eichmann in Jerusalem*, 175.

[12] Raul Hilberg, *The Destruction of the European Jews* (Chicago: Quadrangle Books, 1961), 487–670; Paul Lendvai, *Anti-Semitism Without Jews, Communist Eastern Europe* (Garden City: Doubleday & Co., Inc., 1971), 25.

the Romanian population, however cruel and capricious in the outsider's view, also eludes explanation when seen through the prism of Western ideas of nationalism and anti-Semitism. On the basis of these we would have expected the entire Romanian Jewish community to have been decimated at least to the extent of the communities in Germany and Poland. Obviously we do not expect a state reputedly more anti-Semitic than Hitler's Germany to spare its Jews.[13] This seeming inconsistency between Romania's anti-Semitic reputation and her de facto actions towards her Jewish community has carried over into the post-World War II period. Not only has Communist Romania maintained diplomatic and trade relations with Israel, she has also quietly allowed almost 75 percent of her Jewish population to emigrate to that state. The last statistics which Romania issued detailing its populations by mother tongue and nationality indicated that the Jewish community had declined by some 300,000 people. This represents almost the exact number of Romanian émigrés to Israel.[14] Again, we must recognize Secretary General Nicolae Ceaușescu's desire to steer an independent course in foreign policy from the Soviet Union and to create a positive public relations image where the world Jewish community is concerned.[15] Even so, we would not have expected this mode of conduct from Europe's archetypal anti-Semitic state.

This discrepancy between Romania's well established anti-Semitic heritage and the fate of her Jews in World War II stands out in an even bolder fashion when compared to the Holocaust in fascist Hungary. In stark contrast to the traditional Romanian regime of anti-Jewish disabilities and determined efforts to prevent access to citizenship, the Jewish community in Hungary during the "Golden Era" (i.e., 1867–1918) had assimilated in all areas but that of faith. This process of magyarization produced a Jewish community that rivaled its gentile counterpart in the fervor of its Hungarian nationalism. It had

---

[13] Lendvai, *Anti-Semitism Without Jews*, 332–3.

[14] Ibid., 326–7 & 348; Zvi Zinger, "State of Israel (1948–72), in *Immigration and Settlement* (Jerusalem: Keter Books, 1973), 54–64; *Breviarul statistic al Republicii Socialiste România, 1966* (București: Direcția Centrală de Statistică, 1966), 27–9.

[15] See for example, "A Policy Respectful of Minorities, Impressions of a Delegation of the World Jewish Congress on Their Visit to Romania," *Romania Today*, 1985, nr. 6: 21.

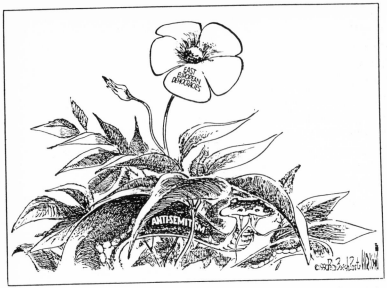

FIGURE II. Cartoon from the Palm Beach [Florida] *Post*. Used with permission of the cartoonist, Don Wright.

had none of the Romanian Jewish experience of dealing with a pervasive, occasionally aggressive anti-Semitism.[16] Yet, despite the vastly different historical traditions regarding anti-Semitism, the Jewish community largely survived in those areas controlled by Romanian forces and perished where the Hungarian fascists held sway. This runs contrary to what we as informed observers would have predicted on the basis of Western theories on the interplay of nationalism and anti-Semitic bias. Though lacking the visceral excesses of the Romanian type, Hungarian anti-Semitism during World War II did permit extensive cooperation between Nazi and Magyar in carrying out an extremely thorough chapter of the Final Solution. And in marked contrast to the Romanian experience the extermination of Hungarian Jews provided the Nazis with full use of all the agencies of state to speed it along. The result,

---

[16] Randolph L. Braham, "The Uniqueness of the Holocaust in Hungary," in *The Holocaust in Hungary Forty Years Later*, Randolph L. Braham & Bela Vago (eds.), (New York: Social Science Monographs, Columbia University Press, 1985), 178; Michael Sozan, "The Jews of Aba," *East European Quarterly*, XX(1986), nr. 4, 181 & 194; Bela Vago, "Contrasting Jewish Leadership in Wartime Hungary and Romania," in *The Holocaust as Historical Experience*, Yehuda Bauer & Nathan Rotenstreich (eds.), (New York: Holmes & Meier Publishers, Inc., 1981), 135.

to use only the example of the bifurcated Transylvania dating from the Vienna Award, was that in the Magyar controlled north four-fifths of the Jewish population disappeared. In the Romanian held south the Jews were left untouched.[17] The Romanian government of Marshal Antonescu showed no reluctance to kill certain types of Jews under specified conditions. But it consistently refused complete cooperation to the Nazis in their efforts to carry out a systematized approach to the Final Solution in the Old Kingdom. Because of this by the end of 1940 the Berlin government viewed Romania—despite the pogroms and Iron Guard—as being "pro-Jewish." Hitler's regime became yet more perturbed upon learning that the Romanians thought of allowing massive Jewish immigration to Palestine (at a quite considerable price per head!). This agitation increased due to the Romanians' categorical rejection of all extreme measures against any Jews who could not be proven to be communists.[18] On some occasions Romanian actions regarding the Jews involved more than merely refusing to kill or export to the extermination camps the hundreds of thousands the Nazis desired. By 1944 an underground smuggling operation, assisted by Romanian peasants as well as others, served as a conduit for a few Jews to escape the Final Solution's operations in the Magyar governed northern portions of Transylvania. These refugees received a conditional sanctuary in the relative safety of the Romanian controlled southern area. This conduct, besides once again being at variance with the assumed pattern of activities and sensibilities for anti-Semites, meant that those aiding in the smuggling ran the serious risk of apprehension and execution. Obviously both the Nazis and the Magyar fascists (who were cooperating so extensively in the completion of the Final Solution in Hungary proper and in northwest Transylvania) knew full well of these actions by the Romanian government and the occasional individual peasant. Indeed, the Hungarian government expressed some considerable discontent over the marked differences in handling the "Jewish Question" in the

---

[17] Braham, "The Uniqueness of the Holocaust in Hungary," 187; Lendvai, *Anti-Semitism Without Jews*, 332.

[18] Andreas Hillgruber, "Anhang I. Die Judenfrage als Problem der Deutsch-Rumänischen Beziehungen," in *Hitler, König Carol und Marschall Antonescu, Die Deutsch-Rumänischen Beziehungen 1938–1944* (Wiesbaden: Franz Steiner Verlag, 1965), 239–42; Vago, "Contrasting Jewish Leaderships," 139.

two territories. What was transpiring under Germany's other ally, Romania, did not correspond to traditional reputations or accepted ideology.[19]

How then can we approach the vagaries of Romanian anti-Semitism so as to explain the unanticipated survival of a majority of the Jewish community that remained under Romanian sovereignty during World War II? In what way do we integrate Antonescu's opportunistic Jewish policy and the legalization of Zionism in Communist Romania immediately after World War II with the horrendous pogroms in Bucharest and Iași in the early 1940s?[20] Initially we must recognize that trying to force the theory and fact of Romanian anti-Semitism on to the procrustean beds of either Western models for bias or the template of Nazism will not suffice. Although containing partial explanations, references to bribe taking and vague notions of "national character,"[21] the supposed increased tolerance of multi-national states and a deficiency in resoluteness on the part of others,[22] and Antonescu's fear that Romania might be occupied as Hungary had been[23] all end up being unsatisfactory. Other areas pronouncedly anti-Semitic and prone to the taking of baksheesh did not shield their Jewish populations as did Romania. This remains so even if we allow for the self-serving and inadvertent nature of the Romanian action. Obviously Antonescu and the Romanian government constantly tried to see which way the winds of war were blowing in order best to ensure their prospects after the conflict, and they found themselves insistently lobbied by foreign governments, the Papacy, and others hoping to mitigate the atrocities being perpetrated on the Jews. Even the tactical nature of Romanian foreign policy in the waning days of the war will not serve as a uniform motive explaining that country's Jewish policies throughout the conflict. Before Stalingrad, cooperating with the Third Reich on this matter as on others would have seemed

---

[19] Ibid., 245; Lendvai, *Anti-Semitism Without Jews,* 333.

[20] Vago, "Contrasting Jewish Leaderships," 141–8.

[21] Ancel, "The Jassy Syndrome (II)," 49–50.

[22] Lendvai, *Anti-Semitism Without Jews,* 333.

[23] Gh. F. Anghelescu & Gh. Buzatu, "Din arhiva istoricâ a României contempo-rane (III): generalul Titus Gârbea despre ultima întrevedere Hitler-Antonescu," *Anuarul Institutul de Istorie și Arheologie "A. D. Xenopol,"* 23(1986): 819–20.

to be the prudent course of action for a vulnerable Balkan state.[24]

Romanian anti-Semitism represents, then a *tertium quid*. Rather than endeavoring to see the Romanian Jewish experience and the amalgam of nationalism and anti-Semitism endemic in that country through twentieth century Western eyes, we must return to the formative period of the mid-nineteenth century. Only in the context of the second half of that century and in the struggle to obtain the country's independence can we accurately discern the lineaments of Romanian anti-Semitism. For at that time there emerged the peculiarly Romanian mixture of ethnic bravado and defensiveness that made anti-Semitism an essential part of being a nationalist. These characteristics coupled with the tensions generated by an immense Jewish immigration from Galicia and Russia produced an anti-Semitism considered normal and fully justified by the intelligentsia. The presence of these émigrés gave a particularly sharp edge to a novel form of anti-Semitic animosity, for they constituted a distinctly different culture not only from the Romanians but also from the Ladino (i.e., Judeo-Spanish) speaking Jewish community long resident in Bucharest.[25] In the period from roughly 1859 to 1914 we will see worked out in some detail all the major characteristics of an anti-Semitism that constituted such an integral part of the intellectual life of that country that being Romanian became synonymous with being an anti-Semite. Furthermore in the process of simultaneously achieving national independence and conceding limited rights (under intense and bitterly resented foreign diplomatic pressures) to this minority, Romania raised the "Jewish Question" to a new level of importance. Those who shaped the national consciousness well into the twentieth century redefined the place Jews might occupy in Romania. Already anti-Semitic at the time of the Congress of Berlin in 1878, the intellectual cum politician became even more so. The most gifted members of the intelligentsia, men who engaged as easily and successfully in politics as in matters of the mind, participated in this ration-

---

[24] Dorian, *The Quality of Witness*, xxxii; Hillgruber, "Anhang I. Die Judenfrage," 245–6.

[25] Nagy-Talavera, *The Green Shirts and the Others*, 44; Henry L. Roberts, *Rumania: Political Problems of an Agrarian State* (New Haven: Yale University Press, 1951), 224.

alized bias. Their patronage gave Romanian anti-Semitism both the currency and respectability of being espoused by the cultural elite. Anti-Semitism for the late nineteenth and twentieth century educated Romanian, then, became a doctrine espoused by some of the most important literary and historical writers in his nation's canon. Rather than being on the intellectual fringe and slightly suspect or unsavory, this anti-Semitism gained prestige and acceptability due to the stature of its spokesmen. One of the members of this intelligentsia to be discussed later wrote that everything that happened on Romanian soil was "providential." Though borrowing from Western sources for his concept he did touch on the fortuitous nature of this anti-Semitism. While not being motivated by humanitarian or moral concerns, this attitude with its roots in the romantic nationalism of the nineteenth century would engender a nondoctrinaire variety of anti-Semitism.[26] This sui generis anti-Jewish prejudice would stand as the backdrop for the survival of most of that community governed by Romania during World War II.

Modernization and the birth of the nation state, with the concomitant impact of Western ideas, gave birth to a significantly different form of anti-Semitism in Romania.[27] This type, though on occasion extraordinarily savage and marked by a self-serving disingenuousness, defined its national goals in a limited manner. That it did so would be critical in the twentieth century for the survival of almost half a million Romanian Jews. Its unusual character would be hidden from view in most instances by a brutality of execution that has led observers over the course of the last hundred years or so to focus on the style rather than substance of what happened. Thus we have the Nazis visiting the scene of the Iași pogrom objecting to the uncivilized manner in which it was perpetrated, while at the same time pressuring Romania to cooperate in the ambitious goals of the Final Solution.[28] And, of course, we have Hannah Arendt's judgment on the preeminent nature of Romanian anti-Semitism (an assessment which seems inexplicable in terms

[26] Joseph Berkowitz, *La Question des Israélites en Roumanie* (Paris: Jouve et Cie, 1923), 677; B. P. Hasdeu, *Istoria Critica a Romanîloru*. II. (București: Typographia Antoniu Manescu, 1874), 10; Hillgruber, "Anhang I. Die Judenfrage," 246.

[27] Eugen Weber, "Romania," in *The European Right* (Berkeley & Los Angeles; University of California Press, 1966), 504.

[28] Nagy-Talavera, *The Green Shirts and the Others*, 334.

of the incomplete results of the Final Solution in Romania) and the implied unfavorable comparison with the Nazi variety. Efficiency and method apparently sanitized the even more absurdly inhumane. However, as Dr. Emil Dorian, one of the most perceptive and articulate of the Jewish witnesses to this tragedy remarked, "You are simply ridiculous if you become selective about the shades of brutality that are to arouse your indignation."[29] Dr. Dorian goes on to point out that for whatever reasons, base or noble, the Romanians did not cooperate in the full execution of the Final Solution as the Nazis wanted and expected them to do. While not demonstrating the courage or idealism of the Danish where the Jews were concerned, neither did the Romanians collaborate as did the Ukrainians, Hungarians, and others. As they had done in the nineteenth century, the Romanians attempted to counterpoise Great Power interests and thereby pursue their own self-interest whenever the Jewish Question came into play. The critical factor of local acquiescence in the sweeping goals of Nazi Germany vis-à-vis the Final Solution did not materialize among the traditionally anti-Semitic Romanians.[30] In Romania the status of the Jewish community had come to be that of an unwelcome but essential bane. As one survivor interviewed for this study explained: "We were *their* [the Romanians'] *Jews*. If any one was going to kill us, it would be them. And they didn't choose to." To understand fully this choice we must now turn to the birth of modern Romania at the Congress of Berlin in 1878 and to the subsequent elaboration of anti-Semitic themes by the Romanian intelligentsia in the period before World War I.

---

[29] Dorian, *The Quality of Witness*, 197. As incredible as it seems, researchers report that in the realm of sadistic cruelty the Gypsy minority in Romania surpassed even the natives in their mistreatment of the Jews; see Ancel, "The Jassy Syndrome (II)," 42.

[30] Elie Wiesel, "Eichmann's Victims and the Unheard Testimony," *Commentary*, 32(1961), nr. 6: 511; Dorian, *The Quality of Witness*, 246.

The Congress of Berlin

With the beginning of the Balkan Crisis in 1875 the Romanians of the United Principalities of Wallachia and Moldavia found themselves on the eve of national independence. United in 1859 as a result of the Peace of Paris (1856) and postwar diplomatic maneuvering, their territories remained an autonomous portion of the Ottoman Empire. Since 1866 the German Prince Carol (i.e., Karl of Hohenzollern-Sigmaringen) had served as their ruler. Even though this prolonged process of war and international negotiation eventually lead to the proclamation of the Kingdom of Romania in 1881, the Romanians felt themselves humiliated and subjected to unwarranted depredations by outsiders. The initial and most pressing problems in this regard resulted quite simply from their geographic situation. Caught between the competing interests of Russia to the north, the Ottoman Empire to the south, and Austria-Hungary to the west, in the late 1870s the Romanians ardently wished to prevent their country from once more becoming a theater of operations in yet another war between the Russians and Ottomans. They desired just as vehemently to acquire their country's independence. Also from the very start of this crisis the Romanian leadership sought ways to frustrate the very clear intent of tsarist Russia to regain the entirety of Bessarabia. Parts of this province had been ceded to the United Principalities as a result of the Crimean War.[1] Unfortunately, while indepen-

---

[1] Ion Bodunescu, *Diplomația românească în slujba independenței* (Iași: Editura Junimea, 1978), 28 & 110; Lothar Maier, "Die Politik Rumäniens in der Orientalischen

13

dence would be gained after a four year military and political struggle, the goals of neutrality and territorial integrity could not be achieved. The United Principalities lay across the traditional and most expeditious southward invasion route for the Russian Empire. The corridor between the Carpathian Mountains and the Black Sea had all the more import for the Russian military enterprise in 1877–1878, since their navy had not yet recovered from the consequences of the 1856 peace treaty. The best to be hoped for, then, from the Romanian stand point revolved around limiting the damage that could be caused by the war. The Danubian Principalities likewise hoped to obtain the optimum diplomatic relationship with the Russian Empire. On 16 April 1877 the Romanian government and the Russians finally signed a convention granting the tsarist army rights of transit across the Principalities (e.g., control of the Romanian railroads for the duration). In return the Romanians received what all recognized as a tenuous commitment to "maintain and defend the actual integrity of Roumania" as well as a vague commitment to Romanian independence.[2] When the Russo-Ottoman war began on 24 April 1877, the Romanian Principalities found themselves immediately occupied by Russian troops. More importantly they plunged into a war of national independence that would imprint on the country an enduring pattern of cultural-political attitudes. The diplomatic impediment to recognition of Romanian independence caused by the presence of several hundred thousand Russian troops would only become obvious at a later date. However, the Romanian authorities discovered at once that the Russians did not wish their active participation in the conflict, treating them as the most junior of allies.[3]

With the Russian convention in place and the Turks distracted by on-going revolts in areas south of the Danube, the Romanian Principalities obviously enjoyed a situation which played

Krise 1875–1878 aus der Sicht der diplomatischen Vertreter Grossbritanniens und Frankreichs in Bukarest," *Südost-Forschungen*, XL(1981), 97.

[2] M. S. Anderson, *The Eastern Question, 1774–1923* (New York: St. Martin's Press, 1966), 194; J. A. R. Marriott, *The Eastern Question*, 4th ed. (Oxford: Clarendon Press, 1963), 334; for the text of this convention see Titu Maiorescu, *Istoria Contimporană a României (1866–1900)*. (Bucureşti: Editura Librăriei Socec & Co., 1925), 116–8.

[3] *Corespondenţa Generalului Iancu Ghica, 2 Aprilie 1877–8 Aprilie 1878*. General Radu R. Rosetti (ed.). (Bucureşti: "Cartea Românească," 1930), 66 & 74–6; Miron Constantinescu et al., *Istoria Romaniei* (Bucuresti: Editura Didactica si Pedagogica, 1969), 356.

to their long term goal of national independence. On 11 and 12 May respectively, the Assembly of Deputies and the Senate formally acknowledged through their votes that a state of war existed with the Ottoman Empire. Subsequently on 21 May the legislature proclaimed Romania's "absolute independence," a stance on the part of that country's nationalistic leaders which would occasion considerable confrontation with the Great Powers. Prince Carol, in his speech of 22 May also stressed this point, equating it to a "national imperative."[4] As we shall see, not only were the Great Powers expressly uneager to grant immediate recognition of Romania's independence, they also intended to impose conditions on the achievement of that much sought after goal. The Romanians in turn interpreted these prerequisites in the offing as an infringement on their dignity and interference in matters exclusively their preserve. Though only a sentiment at the outbreak of the war, by its mid-course Romanian policy would solidify around this motif; namely, that they would accept no decisions to which they were not an active party.[5] With immense popular support for these moves and an overwhelming vote on the part of the legislature, the romantic nationalists wanted immediate, formal acceptance of Romania's nationhood. With patriotic insistence that the Romanian state was now "free and independent," the stage was set for the emergence of a xenophobic reaction. The intellectual elite as well as the ordinary Romanian would be swept along by this nationalistic tsunami. Out of this maelstrom came a definition of who could be a Romanian as well as of what constituted legitimate national interest and unwarranted foreign meddling in the country's domestic affairs. The Romanian definition of independence, therefore, would not allow for the casual treatment by the Great Powers that was forthcoming during the war and the Congress of Berlin. Nor would it tolerate the singling out of a disdained minority such as the Jews for unwonted treatment.[6]

---

[4] Constantinescu, *Istoria României*, 357; "Roumanian Declaration of Independence," *British and Foreign State Papers*, 68 (1876–1877), Foreign Office (London: William Ridgway, 1884), 875.

[5] Nicolae Iorga, *Politica externă a Regelui Carol I* (București: Institutul de Arte Grafice Luceafărul S.A., 1923), 272.

[6] N. Corivan, *Lupta diplomatică pentru cucerirea independenței României* (București: Editura Științifică și Enciclopedică, 1977), 104: Mihail Kogălniceanu, *Opere*, IV (București: Editura Academiei Rupublicii Socialiste România, 1978), 24–5 & 479.

Caught as usual in the contest for supremacy in the Balkans between the Russian and Ottoman empires, the Romanians this time demonstrated a determination if not always a successful capacity to be more than an ancillary factor. Encouraged by the improvement in their army, they felt themselves in a position to aid their own cause. In doing so they thought to precipitate general European recognition of their national existence. Furthermore, the urgency as well as the abruptness of the declaration of their independence symbolized the Romanian effort to salvage their pride after being so brusquely manipulated by Russian interests.[7] The initial check to these ambitions emerged in the Great Powers' decidedly cool reaction to the Romanian importuning of recognition. Taking the tack that this issue must be discussed in the ensuing peace negotiations, the Great Powers sought to protect their interests against the prospect of a greatly magnified Russian presence in southeastern Europe. Obviously, they did not want to contribute to the possible crippling of the Ottoman Empire. They certainly manifested a determined unwillingness to allow matters such as these to be shaped by any agency other than themselves. Besides their strategic concerns, the Great Powers also felt no sympathy for such specific Romanian aims as an international declaration of neutrality for the Principalities.[8] In this otherwise uniformly discouraging diplomatic situation, Italy represented the only marginal element of support for Romanian desires. Long on rhetoric and prudence while continuing almost to the very end of the struggle to be leery of providing demonstrable assistance, the newly independent Italy waxed eloquent on nationalistic themes. In particular, Rome proclaimed both a similarity in the two countries' quest for national independence and her own disinterestedness in the geopolitics of the conflict. Frustratingly for the Romanians and their aspirations, the Italians had a finely developed sense of their

[7] *Independenţa României, Documente II (Partea I), corespondenţâ diplomatică străină 1853–1877*, Vasile Arimia (ed.). (Bucureşti: Editura Academiei Republicii Socialiste România, 1977), 372–3 & 380–2; R. W. Seton-Watson, *A History of the Roumanians* (Hamden: Archon Books, 1963), 334.
[8] Bodunescu, *Diplomaţia românească în slujba independenţei*, 28–9; Richard V. Burks, "Romania and the Balkan Crisis of 1875–78," *Journal of Central European Affairs*, 2 (1942), nr. 2, p. 129; Corivan, *Lupta diplomatică pentru cucerirea independenţei României*, 113 & 149; N. Corivan, "Proclamarea independenţei României şi atitudinea marilor puteri," *Cercetări istorice*, 1977, 335.

own weakness, of their need to follow the lead of the other Great Powers in this matter.[9] Though implicitly approving what the Romanians had done, the government of Italy remained all too conscious of the Russian military presence in the Principalities. Thus, it merely implied future support at the peace conference. The Italian government did counsel the Romanians on the extremely dangerous situation in which the Principalities had become mired. Since the Danube Delta in their estimation represented a strategic goal for several of the Powers, Bucharest's options were few and quite delicately balanced. Most importantly the Italians stressed cooperation with Russia and the stark impossibility of opposing that Empire's designs in the region. This advice on the necessity of capitulating to Great Power demands both in general terms as well as later in terms of specific concessions of territory and minority rights would have to be repeated often before it bore home.[10]

At the beginning of the war, then, the Romanians had to be satisfied with only a verbal demonstration of Italian good-will, though that amounted to considerably more than they found elsewhere. Locked in a combat that meant so much to their future development economically as well as politically, the Romanians welcomed these protestations of benevolence, but they worked desperately to turn them into something more significant diplomatically. What little they could obtain, and that only from the Italians, was a somewhat florid assurance that "no one could turn back a river to its source." The sympathetic Italian government restricted itself to telling the Romanian diplomatic agent in Rome that "Romania was another Italy."[11] More than this it would not and could not accomplish. Having recovered somewhat from their surprise over the impetuousness of the Romanian action, the Italians allowed themselves only an emotional commitment to another Latin civilization. During the war just as later in the midst of the Congress

[9] Constantin Căzănișteanu, "The 1877–1878 War for the Conquest of Romania's State Independence," *Nouvelles Études D'Histoire* (București: Editura Academiei Republicii Socialiste România, 1975), 167; Gr. Chiriță, "Atitudinea puterilor europene față de proclamarea independenței României," *Revista de Istorie*, 30 (1977), nr. 4, 686.

[10] *Documente privind istoria României, Războiul pentru independență*, III. Mihail Roller (ed.). București: Editura Academiei Republicii Populare Române, 1953), pp. 52–4.

[11] Căzănișteanu, "The 1877–1878 War," 173; *Documente privind istoria României, războiul pentru independență*, III, 176 & 421.

of Berlin's discussion on the domestic adjustments demanded of Romania, the government in Rome consistently emphasized to the Romanians that they would have to be reconciled to a level of Italian assistance that remained within "the limits of the possible." Prudence, obviously, would be the order of the day.[12]

The tone for the next four years, then, as well as the margin of success to be enjoyed by the Romanians appeared quite early in both the diplomatic and the military arenas. The government in Bucharest immediately instructed its agents abroad to convey to the various European capitals that it now considered itself to be fully independent. They should request formal recognition. These agents were likewise to advertise the Romanian position regarding the future peace conference; namely, that the Bucharest regime expected to be present and to play a role in determining those matters pertaining to its self-interest. As already mentioned, most European governments reacted with a vague coolness, if not with hostility. The Porte alone demonstrated definitiveness, categorically maintaining its legal rights. France, which would speak up to a limited extent for Romania during the Berlin Congress, remained content to imitate Italy displaying reserve in the affair. The latter state created a virtual foreign policy line out of proclaiming Romania a "second Piedmont," but would proceed no farther than a tacit approval of what the Romanians had done. The government in Bucharest would have to be satisfied for the moment with the Italian assurances that they considered the proclamation of Romanian independence to be "irreversible" even if not canonically accepted by the Great Powers. Though professing to see in the Italian government a steadfast friend, the Romanians would have to wait a considerable while before Rome would be able to discover that elusive but professed occasion to demonstrate its allegiance.[13] No power committed itself to either Romanian independence or even to Romanian participation in the post-war negotiations.

---

[12] *Documente privind istoria României*, III, 109 & 124; *Documente privind istoria Romîniei, războiul pentru independență*, VIII. Mihail Roller (ed.). (București: Editura Academiei Republicii Populare Romîne, 1954), 297.

[13] Bodunescu, *Diplomația românească în slujba independenței*, 111–12; Constantin Căzănișteanu & Mihail E. Ionescu, *Războiul neantîrnării României, 1877–1878* (București: Editura Științifică și Enciclopedică, 1977), 39 & 276–77; Nicolae Iorga, *Politica externă a Regelui Carol I* (București: Institutul de Arte Grafice Luceafărul S.A., 1923), 223–5.

The situation shaped up in a similar fashion where military matters were concerned. Though obviously not a martial power, the United Principalities did possess a modest armed force and therefore a potential to exert considerably more weight in Balkan affairs than had been the case in recent history. The Russians, having initially rebuffed Romanian participation in the war effort, discovered that this small army did have a role to play in the stalled attempt to take the Turkish fortress at Pleven (Plevna) in northern Bulgaria. When that redoubt finally fell on 10 December 1877 after a siege of some five months, the Romanians believed themselves to have been the decisive factor. Certainly they have felt from that day on that their troops had not only played a crucial role in overcoming determined Ottoman resistance, but that this victory constituted one of the most outstanding accomplishments in Romanian history.[14] With the Russo-Turkish war quickly coming to a conclusion after the taking of the stronghold at Pleven, the Romanians prepared for the peace conference. They anticipated, somewhat too sanguinely, far more success in obtaining their dual aims of independence and dignified treatment worthy of a victorious combatant. They experienced immediate disappointment and frustration.

Tsarist Russia, pursuing the exaggerated policies that would generate the Pan-Slavist treaty at San Stefano, treated the Romanians and their sacrifices during the 1877–1878 war with a casual disregard. Not only did the Romanian delegate not gain admittance to the proceedings that produced the armistice (4 February 1878), but Prince Carol had to wait almost two weeks to receive a copy of that document.[15] The discrepancy between the instructions entrusted to the Romanian delegate to the armistice negotiations and the treatment he received presents us with an insight into how the Great Powers felt and dealt with Romania throughout this period. It certainly enlightens us as to why the Romanians came out of the episode feeling disparaged as a loyal ally and greatly aggrieved. For the armistice talks at Kazanlik the Romanian government

---

[14] Corivan, *Lupta diplomatică*, 113–14; *Istoria Romîniei*, IV(1848–1878). P. Constantinescu-Iași (ed.). (București: Editura Academiei Republicii Populare Romîne, 1964), 623; *The Army and the Romanian Society*, Al. Gh. Savu (ed.). (Bucharest: Military Publishing House, 1980), 110.

[15] Anderson, *The Eastern Question*, 199; Bodunescu, *Diplomația românească*, 29.

dispatched Colonel Eraclie Arion, a rather undistinguished officer with no experience or taste for diplomacy.[16] The Romanian government recounted the voluntary nature of the Romanian adherence to the Russian cause during the war and the critical nature of that support. Its directive to Arion then proceeded to insist upon the character of this cooperation as being one between allies who had fought and suffered together. Once having reminded the Russians of this backdrop to the Romanian desire to participate in the armistice negotiations, Arion was to ask for a number of specific items. Besides obvious military considerations such as the occupation by Romanian troops of the Danube border and the eradication of Turkish forts along the river, the Bucharest government wanted recognition of Romania's "absolute and complete independence . . . as a sovereign state." On a somewhat more minor scale, this list of armistice demands also included a very large indemnity to be paid by the Ottoman Empire and a jurisdiction over the Danube delta that conflicted with Russian aims. Arion's instructions concluded with the refrain that would become the anthem of Romanian nationalism, the theme played out by the Romanians in resisting the conditions imposed at Berlin by the Great Powers for her independence. If objections were raised or if these requirements were ultimately rejected, Arion should then advise their Russian allies with the greatest possible resolution that the Romanians would "regard as null and void any actions decided in their name . . . without their direct and formal participation."[17]

The Romanian misapprehension of the situation and their position in it did not correspond at all with Russian intentions. Not only would the specifications carried by Arion not be met, but he would not be admitted to the negotiations. Though phrased diplomatically, the reality possessed sufficient harshness to alert the Romanian government to what lay ahead. The Russian delegation at Kazanlik informed Arion that the armistice constituted a matter for discussion solely between the two principals of the war, Russia and the Ottoman Empire. This being the case, Bucharest should address its concerns to

---

[16] Iorga, *Politica externă*, 276–7; Corivan, *Lupta diplomatică*, 158.

[17] *Documente privind istoria Romîniei, războiul pentru independenţă*, VIII. Mihail Roller (ed.). (Bucureşti: Editura Academiei Republicii Populare Romîne, 1954), 378–81.

St. Petersburg. The pill possessed only slightly more palatability because the Romanians received tactical assurances that they would not be forgotten. Since the Russians knew quite well what Bucharest wanted, the Romanians could rest confident that "Romania's interests were in good hands." Meanwhile, questions of principle and the strategic basis for the final peace treaty would be worked out directly between the two capitals. Actual details such as Arion's list could wait for the peace negotiations. In these preliminaries Russia maintained that she would demonstrate every possible solicitude for Romania and her concerns.[18] Upon contacting St. Petersburg, the Romanians learned that there would be no change in this position. In addition at this juncture the Romanians discovered that the Russians also planned to exclude them from the final peace treaty as well. The Russian position in this instance specified that Romania could play no part in those negotiations, since her independence had not been formally acknowledged by the European powers. The Russian Empire, therefore, would have to bear the burden of representing Romanian interests at the final peace negotiations. The Russians at Kazanlik and later at Adrianople (where the armistice negotiations continued) politely, but steadfastly, held Arion at bay. They declined even to discuss the desires of the Romanian government.[19] Somewhat confusingly Arion reported the absolute refusal of the Russian armistice delegation to deal with him or the Romanian demands in any fashions, but he then went on to relate tenuous evidence that Romania would be allowed to join the negotiations for the peace treaty which convened later at San Stefano. In that context, Romania along with the Russians would regulate such matters as her independence and any compensation that might be forthcoming. As the Romanians learned shortly, Arion had misread the situation and the Russian Empire's designs.[20]

The Russians sat down with the Ottomans to work out the details of what would become the Treaty of San Stefano (signed on 3 March 1878). They showed themselves no more accom-

---

[18] Ibid., 461 & 478–80.

[19] Maiorescu, *Istoria Contimporană a României*, 156–7; Seton-Watson, *A History of the Roumanians*, 338.

[20] *Documente privind istoria României, războiul pentru independență*, IX. Mihail Roller (ed.). (București: Editura Academiei Republicii Populare Romîne, 1955), 64 & 140.

modating towards Colonel Arion and Romanian wishes than they had at the Kazanlik armistice talks. On the one hand the Romanian government asserted its position that, having served as a Russian ally and fought in the war as a distinct entity, it deserved a place at the peace table. St. Petersburg, relying on the 1856 treaty ending the Crimean War, demurred. Romania's status as a fully independent state, and therefore as participant entitled to join in this type of negotiation, must wait upon the decision of the full concert of Europe.[21] In the weeks before the San Stefano treaty was finalized the Romanians protested this treatment, but to no avail. The Russian government retained its posture that Romania could neither take part in the international negotiations nor exercise any other act of sovereignty regarding foreign policy. Until its independence had received the sanction of Europe, such prerogatives would be denied. Romania could play only a consultative role, while the Russian Empire continued to defend that state's best interests. The dialogue between Bucharest and St. Petersburg before San Stefano also became the occasion for further Romanian disillusionment on two other vital points. First, the Russian government vigorously repulsed even preliminary feelers regarding neutrality for Romania. The government in Bucharest received a blunt warning that such neutrality would be perceived as an unequivocal inequity which could not be approved. Russia indicated quite clearly that those states which Romania had to court in order to obtain formal recognition of her independence would back the Russian Empire on this point. Second, the Russians initially promised Romania the sop of acquiring the Ottoman territory between the Danube and the Black Sea (i.e., the Dobrogea) in compensation for her sacrifices during the war. By implication this quittance would likewise expiate the indignity of not having been able to take part in the negotiations ending the war. And then the other shoe fell. At the end of January 1878 the Romanian agent in St. Petersburg informed Bucharest that he had received formal notification that the Russian Empire intended to reclaim that portion of Bessarabia bordering on the Danube delta which it had lost as a result of the Peace of Paris in 1856. On this point the Russians would not yield, protesting that it amounted to "a ques-

---

[21] Kogălniceanu, *Opere,* IV, 25.

tion of honor and national dignity."[22] The Romanians felt compelled to moderate if not abandon their futile pursuit of neutrality, but they would continue through the Congress of Berlin to attempt to prevent the loss of Bessarabia. This became a matter of their nationalistic honor and dignity as well.

The Treaty of San Stefano, concluded between the Russian and Ottoman empires in the first week of March 1878, would necessitate the convening of the Congress of Berlin to renegotiate the status of the large Bulgaria it created. The other Great Powers simply would not tolerate this expression of Pan-Slavic hegemonic tendencies or the increased presence of Russia in southeastern Europe which it portended. The treaty also directly and significantly affected Romania's station. To the great satisfaction of the Romanians Article 5 of the Treaty of San Stefano specified the formal recognition of Romanian independence by the Porte. This article went on to grant Romanian citizens all the rights enjoyed by the citizens of the other European Powers, pending a bilateral treaty between the two states. Having in this fashion fulfilled her promise to watch out for Romania's best interests, Russia then proceeded to guard her own as well. In Article 19 of the treaty the Russians detailed a long list of injuries and losses inflicted by the Ottoman Empire during the 1877–1878 war. These depredations suffered by the Russian Empire amounted, in their calculations, to the sizable sum of 1,410 million rubles. The article quickly proceeded to say that the Russians realized the financial difficulties of the Ottoman Empire at the time. They would be willing to accept a cession of territory for the greater part of the indemnity owed them. Then with great specificity the Russians listed the territory to be ceded, district by district, which amounted to most of the Dobrogea. In conclusion Article 19 stated that the Russian Empire did not wish to annex either the specified territory nor the various islands in the Danube delta. It desired instead to exchange these for the area in Bessarabia given to Romania by the Paris Peace Treaty in 1856. On a more conciliatory note, the article guaranteed that issues of mutual interest between Romania and Russia in regulating the waterway would be governed by a joint commission.[23]

[22] Rosetti, *Corespondenţa Generalului Iancu Ghica*, 123–8 & 149–50.
[23] *Documente privind istoria României*, IX, 360–70.

Quite understandably, after the termination of negotiations at San Stefano the Romanians displayed as much indignation regarding their treatment there and the provisions of Article 19 as they did relief that the Porte had formally recognized their independence. But the independence granted in Article 5 of the Treaty of San Stefano did not compensate for the loss of territory called for in Article 19. Besides a nationwide determination to resist the loss of Bessarabia, the Romanian parliament indulged in some verbal theatrics to vent its anger over the situation. It behaved in this fashion knowing full well that it stood on the diplomatic stage as the weaker party, one most unlikely to prevail. Thus deputies delivered speeches claiming that the damage done to the nation's rights and legitimate interests by the treaty were unconscionable. It would, therefore, be impossible to permit the Russian army to retrace its steps across Romania upon the evacuation of Bulgaria. This reckless assertion, of course, possessed only the character and likelihood of bravado given the pre-war convention between the two countries as well as the overwhelming Russian military presence in the Balkans, but the government felt a compulsion to broadcast its decision to resist such an affront to its sovereignty and to refuse to honor the clause calling for loss of Romanian territory.[24] By this time the Romanians could only hope that the European Powers at Berlin would think better of these provisions and heed their pleas—a forlorn reliance as even the discussions before the Congress of Berlin would demonstrate. Between the signing of the Treaty of San Stefano on 3 March and the beginning of the Congress of Berlin on 13 June, Romania faced an international situation highly unfavorable to her interests. More significantly still her pretensions at this juncture competed with those of the Great Powers. As unjustly as the Romanians found themselves treated after joining in a victorious common cause with the Russians, they could detect among the European states no more than timid support. Alexander II would wait no longer to recover Bessarabia and to eliminate the mortification its loss had caused to the Russian dynasty. No leverage or eloquence available to the Romanians had sufficient impact to alter the diplomatic equa-

---

[24] Maiorescu, *Istoria Contimporană*, 157; Seton-Watson, *A History of the Roumanians*, 341; Corivan, *Lupta diplomatică*, 167–8.

tion to her benefit. St. Petersburg had already made certain of the willingness of the other Great Powers to accept her aggrandizement in this region.[25]

Once again only Italy seemed to offer the Romanians anything more, though as we have seen Rome concentrated on rhetoric rather than on the active support solicited by Bucharest. Having established a diplomatic agent in the Italian capital as early as the spring of 1873, the Romanians cultivated their hosts assiduously. They were just as carefully fed a diet of flowery compliments. On the one hand Italy continued to refer to Romania as "another Italy" and a "second Piedmont," while the Romanians replied in kind calling Rome their "mother." To the gratification of the Romanians the Italian press during the Russo-Turkish war of 1877–1878 made sympathetic references to the two countries' ties of blood and the appropriateness of Romanian claims to independence.[26] While always exhibiting both sympathy and reserve regarding the issue of Romanian independence, the Italian government did on occasion go beyond these platitudes. Most importantly, Rome attempted to delineate for the Romanians the diplomatic realities which Bucharest seemed to wish to sidestep, if not to discount entirely. The Italians consistently protested their desire to assist Romania insofar as that was politically feasible. They likewise cautioned the Romanians that the exclusionary policies towards their Jewish population made for an unfavorable diplomatic climate both in Italy and throughout the rest of Europe. These Italian mentors to the Romanian state kept before their eyes the political reality of the presence of distinguished and fully assimilated Jews in the Italian diplomatic corps, press, and legislature. They hoped to make Bucharest more circumspect and politic in the area of minority rights. Regarding what was to emerge from the Congress of Berlin as the most disturbing single domestic issue for the Romanian government, the question of equal rights and citizenship for its Jewish pop-

[25] N. Iorga, *Histoire des relations russo-roumaines* (Jassy: Éditions du journal "Neamul Românesc," 1917), 362; Corivan, *Lupta diplomatică*, 155; Barbara Jelavich, "Russia and the Reacquisition of Southern Bessarabia 1875–1878," *Südost-Forschungen*, XXVIII(1969), 199–200 & 228.

[26] Raoul V. Bossy, *Politica externă a României între anii 1873–1880 privită dela Agenția diplomatică din Roma* (București: Cultura Națională, 1928), 1; Kogălniceanu, *Opere*, IV, 542; N. Iorga, *Războiul pentru independența României* (București: Cultura Națională, 1927), 60.

ulation, the Italians had even before 1878 put Bucharest on notice as to the inadvisability of these anti-Jewish disabilities.[27]

Since the fall of 1875 Romanian diplomatic agents in Rome had been reporting to the Foreign Minister in Bucharest about the difficulties encountered in trying to obtain a commercial treaty with the Italian government. Such a treaty would possess importance in its own right for economic reasons. The Romanians also wanted it throughout the war period because they believed it would imply recognition of their independence, perhaps even precipitate a formal move on Rome's part. For just as long the Romanian government had heard repeatedly that the treaty would be impossible to accomplish due to the restrictive legislation directed against the Romanian Jewish community. Indeed, Italian diplomatic officials went to great lengths attempting to persuade the Romanians that tolerance and equality of rights for the Jews possessed both theoretical merit and diplomatic advantage. The Italians sought to convince the authorities in Bucharest that many reasons counseled the assimilation of the Romanian Jewish community. They specifically cited the examples of both France and Italy to demonstrate the benefits to society at large from such a policy. On a more practical note, they warned the Romanians that the commercial treaty could not be signed as long as even an appearance existed that Italian citizens of Jewish descent trading in Romania might fall under the jurisdiction of those anti-Semitic disabilities. No Italian government could or would permit a distinction to be made between those of its citizens who were Christian and those who were Jewish.[28]

The government in Rome seized upon this situation as an opportunity to fulfill its promise to find an occasion to assist Romania, but the aid rendered did not come in the mode imagined by the Romanians or in a palatable form. Rather the Italians made the argument that the Romanians had committed a singular error in this regard, one leading the rest of Europe to view them as intolerant. As far as domestic politics were a factor, the Romanians received a blunt warning that the Italian

---

[27] N. Iorga, *Correspondance diplomatique roumaine sous le roi Charles Ier (1866–1880).* Deuxième édition (Bucarest: Bibliothèque de l'Institut pour l'Étude de l'Histoire Universelle, 1938), 262, 266, & 268–9.

[28] Bossy, *Politica externă a României,* 125, 135, & 138–40.

newspapers would continue to fulminate against Romanian bigotry. In this climate, even if not already predisposed to do so for humanitarian reasons, the Italian parliament would never accept a treaty distinguishing between types of Italian citizens. The Italian presentation of this issue to the Romanian diplomatic agent in Rome was of such a forceful nature that he advised his government that this "burning question" should be avoided. Interestingly, in spite of this categorical stance of the Italian government in protecting its own citizens, it did make one theoretical concession to the Romanian point of view on anti-Jewish disabilities. This allowance would be seized upon later and made a cardinal element in the Romanian effort to justify its constitutional restrictions on Jewish rights and citizenship. The Italians, in stressing the "Latin" nature of the Romanians and the oft repeated similarity to themselves, admitted that certain constraints might be imposed on Jews emigrating to Romania from Galicia and Podolia. Since this portion of the Jewish population in Romania constituted a "germanizing" force likely to have a detrimental effect on the Latin character of Romania and its culture, it would be proper to maintain some qualifications as to their civil and legal status.[29]

Through the spring of 1878 as the time for Congress of Berlin neared, the Italian government continued its policy of what has been termed "platonic" support of the Romanian cause. By 23 March the Romanians had been able to assuage Italian sensibilities sufficiently that the commercial convention was finalized. Despite the low profile posture it had chosen to take, Rome in the Romanian view had implicitly recognized Bucharest's independence and somewhat strengthened the Danubian state's bargaining position.[30] Just as significantly this interchange with the Italians had been for the Romanians a foretaste of what was to come in its confrontation with the Great Powers at Berlin. In rationalizing a set of answers to the Italians' indictment on the Jewish question, they began the process of constructing a public relations platform. They also began the elaboration of a theoretical basis for continued selectivity

---

[29] *Documente privind istoria României, războiul pentru independență*, III, 422–24.

[30] Corivan, *Lupta diplomatică*, 178; Ion Ionașcu, Petre Bărbulescu, & Gheorghe Gheorghe, *Tratatele internaționale ale României, 1354–1920* (București: Editura Științifică și Enciclopedică, 1975), 226–7.

in granting the privileges of Romanian citizenship. The initial Romanian response in these conversations with the Italian government stressed that the legal disabilities experienced by the Jews in Romania had nothing to do with religion. Rather they were imposed for economic and national reasons, which had no relationship to sectarian factors. The Romanians waxed adamant that there existed no hatred of Jews, no medieval sentiment, and no question of the attitudes that lead to pogroms. They merely wished to preserve the national culture and economic resources. Their rejoinder to Italian press coverage and to the admonishments of some Jewish rights advocates within Italian diplomatic circles was characteristically Levantine. These pressures originated solely in the partisan influence of the Jewish segment of the population. Ominously for subsequent developments they made the point that a small, relatively weak country like Romania must resent foreign intrusion in its domestic affairs. Romanians could resolve their own problems without the humiliation of foreign meddling in their concerns.[31] In the face of enormous diplomatic pressures and under threat of possible denial of Great Power recognition of their independence, the Romanians would cling to and elaborate on these themes. Even when forced to concede certain constitutional reforms in the area of minority rights, they would persist in interpreting and enforcing those legal concessions in a manner consistent with their original presentation to the Italians.

As 13 June and the opening of the Congress of Berlin approached, the Romanian Foreign Minister (Mihail Kogălniceanu, 1817–1891) worked feverishly to gain formal recognition of his country's independence. For by now this matter had become more than one of just national pride and diplomatic niceties. In his review of Romania's tactical situation Kogălniceanu had clearly perceived that European recognition of Romanian independence, Romania's subsequent ability to participate at the Berlin Congress, and therefore his ability to preserve the country's territorial integrity were necessarily and closely linked. Late in the spring of 1878 he communicated his desperation to his diplomatic agents in the major capitals.

---

[31] Bossy, *Politica externă a României*, 134–6 & 138–41; Iorga, *Politica externă a Regelui Carol I*, 319.

Even in the event of not obtaining European-wide recognition of Romania's independence he could not facilely accept exclusion from the Congress. The Romanian government's stance would continue to be that nothing could be decided about Romania without Romania's active participation. Though acknowledging that they could not be seated at the Congress in the same capacity as one of the Great Powers, the Romanians did insist on being treated as a state having an essential role to play in the proceedings.[32] In the futile hope of effectively engaging in the negotiations at Berlin, Kogălniceanu drew up a memorandum containing Romania's basic aims. Besides desiring specific rights along the Danube estuary and a share of any Ottoman indemnity proportional to their participation in the war, Kogălniceanu also voiced the Romanians' brash demand that the Russian army not be allowed to use their country as a thoroughfare. More importantly, the memorandum contained Bucharest's request for solemn recognition of its independence with full national territorial integrity and internationally guaranteed neutrality.[33] Even if seated at Berlin, such a shopping list would have been far too ambitious for a Balkan state with limited resources, just debuting on the international scene. Moreover, on a more pragmatic plane, Kogălniceanu and his government soon found themselves fighting a battle affecting domestic as well as foreign policy affairs.

Informed by St. Petersburg that the retrocession of Bessarabia comprised a matter of Russian national commitment, the Romanians had seen this design written into the Treaty of San Stefano.[34] Now they braced themselves for a struggle in the arena of Berlin. When their consultative delegation did eventually depart for the German capital, it did so with the most categorical of instructions from both houses of the Romanian parliament. Echoing the deeply felt sentiment of the nation, the parliament doggedly stipulated that Bessarabia not be ceded even in exchange for the Dobrogea. This injunction was, indeed,

---

[32] *Independența României, Documente*, IV (*Documente Diplomatice, 1873–1881*). A. Gr. Paraipan, A. N. Popescu, & C. I. Turcu (eds.), (București: Editura Academiei Republicii Socialiste România, 1978), 343; Corivan, *Lupta diplomatică*, 160.

[33] Corivan, *Lupta diplomatică*, 181.

[34] *Documente privind istoria României, războiul pentru independență*, IX, 367; *Corespondența Generalului Iancu Ghica*, 128.

the last and most unequivocal statement conveyed to them before the Congress. Obviously it ran in the face of Great Power purposes. Similarly the Romanians had also been made aware by the Italian government that the demand for neutrality, and with it the coveted freedom from armies transiting their territory, remained a forlorn hope. Since in 1875 the Italians had advised that neutrality did not offer them the best protection, Romania would be better off remaining under the guarantee of the Great Powers, even if that status did savor of a certain degree of tutelage.[35] What the Romanians were probably not as well steeled for was the imbroglio over anti-Jewish disabilities, although the Italians had also alerted them to humanitarian sensitivities in this regard on the part of the major European states. Despite Romanian protestations that their restrictive legislation reflected only social and economic attitudes, for over a decade prior to the Congress of Berlin Europe had been willing to place scant credence in Romania's arguments. Though in the overall diplomatic equation of the Congress this did not constitute a major element, it did assume extensive proportions for Romania both there and in subsequent years. For it placed Romania outside the community of civilized nations. Only Russia shared a common interest in this area and likewise the same accusation of a reprehensible posture towards a "racial"[36] minority. Thus whatever slight leverage Romania might have possessed in seeking to acquire the prizes on Kogălniceanu's list was eroded considerably. In the eyes of the European Great Powers Romania lost stature and any chance of exerting moral suasion.[37]

In these none too favorable circumstances, then, the Romanian consultative delegation of Prime Minister Ion C. Brătianu (1821–1891) and Foreign Minister Kogălniceanu left for the German capital to present Bucharest's case. Disappointingly from their point of view, they would not be party to the

---

[35] Titu Maiorescu, *Discursuri parlamentare*, II(1876–1881). (Bucureşti: Editura Librăriei Socecŭ & Comp., 1897), 183–4; Gheorghe Platon, "Afirmarea suveranităţii României în preajma războiului din 1877–1878. Mărturii din arhivele Belgiei," *Studii şi Materiale de Istorie Modernă*, V(1975), 184.

[36] Nineteenth century Romanian anti-Semites employed the term "*rasă*" (race) as the rough equivalent of "nationality." The word did not denote the same values nor have the overtones it came to possess in the twentieth century.

[37] W. N. Medlicott, "The Recognition of Roumanian Independence, 1878–1880," *Slavonic Review*, XI(1933), 355–56; *Documente privind istoria României, războiul pentru independenţă*, III, 422–4.

actual determinations but merely allowed to offer a memorial summarizing their arguments. In the end they would modify no delegate's views. The decisions of the Great Powers on Danubian issues would result in the same resolutions as if Brătianu and Kogălniceanu had never been present; namely, Romania's independence would be conditional waiting on cession of Romanian territory and significant alteration in the country's constitutional structure. They had no positive impact and, indeed, had to report home with even worse news from the Romanian point of view than the exchange of Bessarabia for the Dobrogea.[38] Romania's concerns, then, became lost in the constellation of Great Power ambitions. With only Italy as an occasional advocate, Brătianu and Kogălniceanu could do little. For Italy would carry little weight at Berlin, influencing the Romanian issue only in a tangential fashion. Italy for her part followed the lead of Great Britain at the Congress. Among the Great Powers with something essential at risk, the British obviously wanted to maintain the territorial integrity of the Ottoman Empire as a counterweight to Russian influence in the region. Insofar as preventing preponderant Russian impact on the lower Danube and preserving the balance of power were compatible with Romanian aims, then the British would acquiesce in Romanian independence. France, like Great Britain, wished to protect the status quo in Eastern Europe as well as to uphold the principle of collective guarantees. Her interests too would be best served by no one power having hegemonic influence on the emerging Romanian state.[39] Though some humanitarian concerns would surface at the Congress of Berlin, of the remaining Great Powers only one would have any pragmatic compulsion for manipulating Romanian interests. Russia would be satisfied with regaining Bessarabia; the Ottoman Empire had already recognized Romanian independence; and Austria-Hungary would follow Berlin's lead. And so it fell to that capital's leader to decide the outlines of Romania's appearance as a completely accepted member of the European community. In this context the issue of Jewish rights, whether for German citizens working in the Danubian

[38] Petre Bărbulescu (ed.), *Reprezentanţele diplomatice ale României*, I (Bucureşti: Editura Politică, 1967), 22–3.

[39] Ciachir, *Războiul pentru independenţa României*, 232; Iorga, *Politică externă a Regelui Carol I*, 304; Maier, "Die Politik Rumäniens in der Orientalischen Krise," 84.

Principalities or members of the Romanian Jewish community, assumed a highly visible but distinctly secondary role in the diplomatic reckonings of the Congress. The Germans led by Otto von Bismarck had as a more importunate objective the extrication of the immense sums rashly invested in Romanian railroads.

As chancellor of Imperial Germany, Bismarck served both as host for the Congress and as its chief figure. His eagerly sought after goal at the conference lay in preparing the way for the resurrection of the Three Emperors' League. With this alliance once more in place, Bismarck envisioned Germany attaining a dominant position on the continent, one allowing the German Empire to eclipse both Russia and Great Britain. In his extensive and long-term efforts in this direction Bismarck had received the assistance of a German banker of Jewish extraction, Gerson von Bleichröder. Bleichröder functioned as a most helpful means of communication with both London and Paris as well as an effective factotum to Bismarck on matters of German national interest in the financial arena. In this link between Bleichröder and Bismarck Romania's future came into question not only because of the question of Jewish rights but also of the heavy investment by prominent Germans in the Romanian railroad system. The Jewish banker and others had considerable holdings in these lines and now wished to see them repurchased by the Romanian government. This the Romanians refused to do in a manner acceptable to Berlin. In the end Bismarck would establish a diplomatic linkage between the sale of the Romanian railways, the condition of the Romanian Jewish community, and the possibility of Bucharest's independence being recognized by the concert of European states. The Chancellor, then, originated the idea of championing the issue of Jewish rights to bring pressure to bear upon the Romanian government. He, like the Italians, also had the additional motivation of a parliament adverse to a commercial connection with a state whose laws might discriminate against German citizens on the basis of the individual's faith.[40]

---

[40] Martin Winckler, "Bismarcks Rumänienpolitik und die Durchführung des Artikels 44 des Berliner Vertrages (1878–1880)," Ph.D. Dissertation, Ludwig-Maximilians-Universität zu München, 1951, 96; Burks, "Romania and the Balkan Crisis of 1875–78," 318.

In the summer of 1878, therefore, the question of the denial of citizenship rights to Romanian Jews became a peripheral but unavoidable topic of discussion at the Congress of Berlin. The majority of principal players at the conference had, at best, a visionary regard for the community in question. Bismarck, of course, intended to garner very specific, concrete results in the financial and diplomatic areas. The *quid pro quo* for Bleichröder was to be found in the pressure brought to bear on the Romanian government for the liberalization of the Romanian constitution of 1866. That document would presumably be altered in such a manner that the Jews of Romania would no longer be victimized by unequal treatment. By the same token, the degree to which the leverage of the Jewish issue might be employed by Bismarck depended on his perception of what progress had been made towards the repurchase by the Romanian government of the German held railroads. Whatever may have been Bleichröder's insight into the use Bismarck would ultimately make of the Romanian Jewish issue, he entered the period of the Congress deeply suspicious of Romanian goodwill. In the evaluations he delivered to the Jewish communities of Western Europe he emphatically stressed that neither the Romanian government nor the populace at large possessed any inclination to accord equality to their Jews. Of great significance for the final outcome of this question was Bleichröder's opinion that unless Europe brought significant, unceasing force to bear upon Bucharest there would be no real improvement in the condition of that nation's Jewish community. Sadly, he would be proved all too prescient on this point. But in 1878, before the opening session of the Congress, Bismarck's commitment to exercise the full weight of Germany's diplomatic influence to this end seemed to promise success. Unfortunately, Romania's obduracy would be underestimated as would the ingenuity of the anti-Semitic intelligentsia of that nation. For in the beginning of this diplomatic struggle linking Romanian independence and full civil rights for the Jews, even giving lip service to equality stuck in the throats of the fervent anti-Semites. In the end mouth honor was all that could be obtained.[41]

---

[41] Fritz Stern, *Gold and Iron. Bismarck, Bleichröder, and the Building of the German Empire* (New York: Vintage Books, 1979), 377; Carol Iancu, *Les Juifs en Roumanie (1866–*

Since Romanian independence along with the corollary issues of the Bessarabia's status and anti-Jewish disabilities did not stand center stage at the Congress of Berlin, some two weeks passed before the question of Romanian participation arose. Then on 29 June Lord Salisbury,[42] speaking for the British delegation, brought up the topic of whether or not the Congress should hear Bucharest's position on these and other matters of concern to the Danubian capital. The Russian delegates and Bismarck opposed permitting the Romanians to voice their appeal. Russia's adamant stance might well be expected given the goal of regaining Bessarabia. Bismarck expressed a willingness to accede to this courtesy, but only if his colleagues from the other missions thought it proper. In the end the Austrians, Italians, and French sided with the British, voting to hear from the Romanian Prime Minister and Foreign Minister. William Henry Waddington, France's foreign minister, possibly echoing Bleichröder's anxieties over Romanian goodwill, anticipated the crux of the matter. He emphasized that this act of consideration might motivate the Romanians to accept more readily the decisions of the Congress. Though this confidence would prove to be illusory, the Romanians were granted an audience for the next session of the Congress.[43]

Finally on 1 July the two Romanian ministers made their brief, inauspicious appearances at the Congress. Nothing they read in their memoranda came as a surprise disclosure to the delegates, since they simply reiterated the Romanian proposals from the period before San Stefano.[44] Kogălniceanu, speaking at more length than his prime minister, dealt primarily with the territorial issues, especially with the possible alienation of Bessarabia. As to be expected he likewise addressed the primary goal of independence as well as the unattainable one of an internationally guaranteed neutrality for Romania. Brătianu read an even shorter statement focusing on Romanian territorial integrity. Having endured this unhappy experience, the two Romanian politicians were dismissed so that the Con-

---

1919), de l'Exclusion à l'Emancipation (Aix-en-Provence: Éditions de l'Université de Provence, 1978), 155–6.

[42] Robert Arthur Talbot Gascoyne-Cecil, Secretary for Foreign Affairs in 1878.

[43] "Protocole No. 9. Séance du 29 Juin 1878," *Nouveau recueil général de Traités, et autres actes relatifs aux rapports de droit international*. Continuation du grand recueil de G. Fr. de Martens. III (Göttingen: Librairie de Dieterich, 1878), 252–3.

[44] Seton-Watson, *A History of the Roumanians*, 343.

FIGURE III. Mihail Kogălniceanu. From: *Mihail Kogălniceanu* in *Editura Enci-clopedică Română.*

gress could begin its discussions of their country's status. Inter-estingly neither man spoke to the Jewish issue or in any way tried to preempt what would become the central legal and dip-lomatic qualification impeding recognition of Romania's inde-pendence.[45] Ultimately their trip to Berlin prevented neither

---

[45] "Protocole No. 10, Séance du 1er Juillet 1878," *Nouveau recueil général de Traités,* III, 358–62.

the loss of Bessarabia nor the linking of Romanian independence with the quandary of Jewish rights. Indeed, the Romanian perception in both the nineteenth and twentieth centuries
has centered on the West's obtuseness. Thus the Western Great
Powers impolitically refused to weigh the effects of what the
anti-Semites claimed to be a recent and massive Jewish immigration into the Danubian state.[46] Indicative once again of the
motivation for Bucharest's final acceptance of the Congress
of Berlin's decrees was the fact that Brătianu and Kogălniceanu
left the German capital obliged to report a Hobson's choice
to their government; namely, no recognition by the European
concert of powers (despite their former sovereign's having
already granted this) or what they believed to be a fundamental
alteration in Romania's socio-legal fabric by removing anti-
Jewish disabilities.[47]

With the Romanian ministers out of the room, Chancellor
Bismarck began the discussion by remarking to the other delegates that they were to decide not just if, but also under what
conditions, Romanian independence should be recognized.
He specifically reminded them that, while that country was
now united and had signed commercial treaties implying Euro-

---

[46] As will be shown later in this study, the Romanian position posited that no
native Jews existed in the Principalities. The authorities in Bucharest as well as the
many vocal anti-Semites consistently maintained this claim, despite the centuries-
long presence of Jewish communities in the country. The definitive statement from
the Romanian point of view can be found in *La Roumanie et les Juifs* by Verax [Radu
Rosetti], (Bucarest: I. V. Socecu, 1903). The figures presented here will help the outsider to gauge more accurately the professed demographic motivations of Romanian
anti-Semitism throughout the period leading up to World War I. They certainly expli-
cate the depth of Moldavian anti-Jewish sentiment and the disproportionate representation of inhabitants of that province among the anti-Semitic intelligentsia. Verax,
speaking for this lobby, set the 1803 Jewish population in Moldavia at 2 percent, while
the 1859 and 1899 censuses produced figures of 9 percent and 10.7 percent respectively (pp. 7, 32, & 38). More startling still from the Romanian perspective were the
percentages for the population of Iaşi, the Moldavian capital; namely, the Jewish pro-
portion of inhabitants grew to 47 percent by 1859 and 51.2 percent by 1899 (pp. 33 &
39). Interestingly also, Verax like his anti-Semitic predecessors at the time of independence continued to maintain that this Jewish population consisted almost entirely
of immigrants from Russia, Poland, and Galicia (pp. 55–6 & 369). He likewise insisted
that the sole intent of Romanian anti-Semitism resided in a nonviolent effort to keep
the Romanians dominant in their own state. But he qualified this position with the
caveat that where the essential concerns of the state and the legal protections afforded
the Jewish minority came into conflict, then "the welfare of the state is the supreme
law" ("Salus rei publicae suprema lex" [sic]; 370). With this quotation he summed up
not only his own attitude, but also the most pervasive motif of Romanian anti-Semitism.

[47] George I. Brătianu, *La politique extérieure du Roi Charles I-er de Roumanie* (Bucureşti:
"Cartea Românească," 1940), 16.

pean acceptance of that condition, the Peace of Paris (1856) had not specifically allowed for such unification. This time Bismarck wished to see matters handled a bit more neatly and emphasized that only Europe had the right to sanction Romania's independence. Bismarck set the tone as well as direction for the subsequent deliberations. He proposed that the import and multilateral nature of the decision to grant independence be brought home by setting certain stipulations; i.e., those already determined by the Congress for the recognition of Serbian sovereignty.[48] For Romania's position coming out of the Congress of Berlin this move of Bismarck's proved decisive. Furthermore, it immediately summoned up the one critical point that both Brătianu and Kogălniceanu had left out of their addresses to the Congress. In the session of 28 June, France's Foreign Minister Waddington had proposed that Serbia be granted independence only upon acceptance of the condition that all her inhabitants "whatever their religion, enjoy a complete equality of rights." The raising of this point in the earlier sitting brought forth a touchy response from Prince Aleksandr Mikhailovich Gorchakov, the Russian foreign minister, who displayed considerable defensiveness given the status of that empire's Jewish population. But despite demeaning rationalizations on the subject of the impact made by the Jewish community as well as distinctions between Western and Eastern Jews (the very arguments that the Romanians would later use in an attempt to avoid the full consequences of the Congress), the Russian delegation eventually followed the French lead. Waddington urged the delegates to seize this opportunity to profess publicly the principle of religious toleration. The Russians quickly modified their stand to indicate no opposition to this innocuous generality, while Bismarck proclaimed Germany's unremitting commitment to champion religious liberty. Italy, already so disposed and having counseled the Romanian diplomatic agent in Rome on this very point, went along.[49]

With this congenial proposal of Bismarck's on the floor, Waddington picked up his theme from the previous exchange on

---

[48] "Protocole No. 10," *Nouveau recueil général de Traités,* III, 362.

[49] "Protocole No. 8. Séance du 28 Juin 1878," *Nouveau recueil général de Traités,* III, 341–2.

Serbia urging the Congress to impose the same preconditions on Romania. The French foreign minister, acknowledging the Russian attempts at vindication and anticipating those which would be forthcoming from the Romanians, conceded that there might be local difficulties in the region. However, he urged in the name of France that the noble principles of equal rights and religious liberty must take precedence over these national singularities. Waddington scored a telling shot pointing out that it would be inappropriate for a European state not to recognize rights accorded even to the subjects of the Ottoman sultan. If Romania desired the security and dignity of belonging to the family of European nations as an independent political entity, then she must comport herself as a civilized country. If some slight inconvenience arose in doing so, that comprised part of the price of independence. At the end of the session Great Britain, Austria-Hungary, France, Germany, and Italy all voted unconditionally to demand of Romania that she accord her Jewish population full political rights and religious liberties. The Tsarist empire accepted the French humanitarian position, but then on a more prosaic note stipulated that its recognition of Romanian independence would be subordinated to the cession of certain territories (i.e., Bessarabia).[50]

Motivated by the idealism of the French and the political action of organized Jewish groups in the West, the Congress of Berlin decreed that the Romanian legal disabilities dating back to the 1860s would have to be abolished. In question were the revised Civil Code of 1864 and the constitution of 1866. The new code promulgated in 1864, while not perhaps up to Western standards, did provide an equality of sorts for the Romanian Jewish community, at least on paper. Indeed, in as much as Article 16 permitted the naturalization of Jews, it was wholeheartedly welcomed by that community as a distinct improvement in its lot. In reality, however, an individual Jew found it extraordinarily difficult, if not impossible, to obtain naturalization under the more liberal code of 1864. Between the passage of the law and the ascension to the throne of Prince Carol in 1866 not a single person did manage to obtain naturalization under its provisions. More ominously, the simple fact that a seeming breach in the legal barriers to citizenship

---

[50] "Protocole No. 10," *Nouveau recueil général de Traités*, III, 362–3.

had been opened to the Jewish community aroused intense hostility on the part of pronounced Romanian nationalists.[51]

The center of controversy and the focal point in the contest over Romanian independence resided, however, in Article 7 of the constitution of 1866. There, after specifying that legislatively enacted civil laws would govern the acquisition of Romanian citizenship, the constitution went on to declare that "Only foreigners of Christian rites may obtain naturalization." As we will see in more detail in the discussion of the debates in the Romanian parliament this specification in the 1866 constitution not only violated Western notions of religious tolerance, but by implication read into law the nationalist's precept that there existed no Romanian citizens of Jewish origin. All Jews were aliens. This attitude coupled with the complete failure of the naturalization article in the Civil Code of 1864 helps explain both the resolute quality of the anti-Romanian agitation by Jewish organizations[52] in Western Europe and the well justified suspicions regarding Romanian goodwill. Bleichröder's role as an adviser to Bismarck and his caution on the subject of Bucharest's attitudes assumed paramount importance in attempting to deal with the situation.[53] To add to Romania's awkward situation, in terms of public relations as well as of diplomacy, her bearing in this dilemma compared most unfavorably with that of Serbia. Though the Congress had some doubts as to what Serbia contemplated due to the phrasing of her commitment, the Serbs immediately pledged their loyal adherence to the decisions made at Berlin and specifically to abolish all restrictions on their Jewish community. To no avail might the Romanians remonstrate that the Jewish population in Serbia was far smaller in absolute numbers and nothing like the percentage of the populace that its counterpart was in Romania. Bucharest gave the distinct impression, and would continue to do so throughout the eighteen month tug-of-war until formally recognized as independent, of attempting to frus-

---

[51] Constantin C. Giurescu. *Viaţa şi opera lui Cuza Vodă* (Bucureşti: Editura Ştiinţifică, 1966), 42–4 & 311–12; Iancu, *Les Juifs en Roumanie*, 59–60.

[52] Both before and during the Romanian independence impasse the "Alliance Israélite Universelle" played the most active, though not ultimately an effective, role. See pp. 60, 65, 136, 142, & 144.

[53] Frédéric Damé, *Histoire de la Roumanie Contemporaine* (Paris: Germer Baillière et Cie, 1900), 425–6; Iancu, *Les Juifs en Roumanie*, 155–6.

trate the clear intent of the Congress relative to the Jewish issue. In this instance the misgivings over Serbia's true intentions occasioned Bismarck's famous declaration, aimed more at Romania than Serbia, that no reservations or disingenuousness would be permitted to undermine the determinations arrived at by the Congress. The Romanians were given sharp notice, therefore, that Bismarck intended to have his way on this subject. His emphatic observation also came in the context of the Congress formally adopting the protocol dealing with Romania's internal situation.[54]

The issue of Bessarabia which had been the main concern of Romanian diplomatic efforts at the Congress was settled even more expeditiously. On 29 June the Russian chief negotiator, Count Petr Andreevich Shuvalov, stressed that the reacquisition of this area did not constitute a matter of self-interest or national ambition. Rather, as had earlier been stated to the Romanians, the Russian Empire viewed the retrocession of Bessarabia as "a question of honor." That this constituted an issue of honor rather than of strategic advantage formed the basis for the Russian decision not to seek more definitive control of the lower Danube and the delta. Furthermore, Shuvalov offered the aside that Romania would be acquiring an enormous territory in the Dobrogea, a great prize commensurate with her sacrifices in the late Ottoman war. Bismarck, for one, quickly backed the Russian position.[55] Having been put on notice by the Russians that they expected no other Great Power to back Romania's efforts to retain Bessarabia, the Congress as a whole acquiesced in St. Petersburg's demand. France and Italy did, however, advocate granting Romania a larger share of the Dobrogea in compensation. Waddington, in particular, wanted the Romanians to be aware of French largess. He advised that the more generous portion be awarded, which would give Romania an additional port on the Black Sea, as a means of enticing a more willing acceptance of the loss of Bessarabia and the other determinations of the Congress. Privately he counseled his government that this move would also put more distance between Russia and Bulgaria. This increased

---

[54] "Protocole No. 12. Séance du 4 Juillet 1878," *Nouveau recueil général de Traités*, III, 380.

[55] "Protocole No. 9," *Nouveau recueil général de Traités*, 355–7; "Protocole No. 10" *Nouveau recueil général de Traités*, 364–5.

separation he believed to be much in the interest of Europe.[56] Thus on 1 July the French foreign minister made a vigorous, public appeal to the Russian delegation to deal more equitably with a Romania which had, in Waddington's words, "been treated a bit harshly." The segment of Dobrogea originally intended for Romania was not sufficient according to his view. He also offered the bait of continued French diplomatic pressure on the Romanians to accept the loss of Bessarabia as an unavoidable sacrifice but one that could be turned to her advantage. Under this prodding Shuvalov committed Russia to a redefinition of the Romanian-Bulgarian frontier in the southern Dobrogea. The other members of the Congress then agreed to a border that placed the port of Mangalia within Romania.[57] Despite this singular effort by the French, the Romanians would be bitterly disappointed with the outcome of the Congress and equally resolved to oppose the implementation of its decrees in every possible fashion.

When the Congress of Berlin ended on 13 July, the stage was set for what the Romanian government would view as an unwarranted intervention in that country's domestic politics and socioeconomic order on behalf of the Jewish community. The populace at large displayed an even greater sense of outrage. The loss of Bessarabia, of course, evoked enormous discontent. It also created a permanent distrust of Russia which would persist long after the Congress and the ensuing battle over Romanian independence. After the proclamation of the Kingdom of Romania in 1880, this recasting of her northeastern boundary constituted the dominant factor in the formulation of an anti-Russian strand in Bucharest's foreign policy. Those actually witnessing what had transpired reacted with a deep sense of mortification at how cavalierly Romania had been treated by Europe as a whole and by her erstwhile ally Russia in particular. Kogălniceanu, reporting to Prince Carol two days after the termination of the Congress, deemed the final redaction of the conference's decrees to be a significant encroachment on Romania's sovereignty and a major injury to her dignity.[58]

---

[56] *Documents diplomatiques français (1871–1914).* 1re série (1871–1900), V. 2 (Paris: Imprimerie Nationale, 1930), 344–7; Ciachir, *Războiul pentru independența Romqniei,* 269.
[57] "Protocole No. 10," *Nouveau recueil général de Traités,* 363–5.
[58] *Aus dem Leben König Karls von Rumänien; Aufzeichnungen eines Augenzeugen.* IV (Stuttgart: Cotta'sche Buchhandlung, 1900), 81; Marriott, *The Eastern Question,* 344;

The origins of this agitation as well as of the political turmoil that would grip Romania for the next year and a half are to be found in Articles XLIII-XLVI of the Congress's proceedings. Article XLIII presented the Romanians with the basic framework for their upcoming parliamentary maneuverings and the ideological context in which their nationalism would ferment; namely, that the Powers recognized her independence only on the premise of her acceptance and execution of the conditions specified in the other three articles. Subsequently Articles XLV and XLVI carefully delineated the cession of Bessarabian territory to Russia by Romania and of the Dobrogea by the Ottoman Empire to Romania. Though Romania received Mangalia as promised by the Congress under French urging, this outcome was exactly what the Romanian delegates had been mandated by their legislature to prevent.[59] As might be expected, Russian territorial aggrandizement generated considerable resentment. More significantly, Romanian governmental and popular reactions to the Powers' dictation on Jewish rights demonstrated a depth of intellectual as well as visceral opposition that exceeded expectation and eventually the Powers' coercive capabilities.

Article XLIV, then, became the focus of Romanian recalcitrance and of the Western powers' determination to have their ways, either humanitarian or self-interested. For Article XLIV categorically decreed that henceforth no difference of religious belief or sect could preclude an individual from the enjoyment of civil or political rights. Furthermore, all members of the Romanian populace now would possess the right of admission to any and all professions or types of work (public and private) as well as the option to choose the locality where they might wish to find employment. Religious tolerance was defined as the right of every resident in Romania to freedom of conscience and the liberty to practice his faith publicly. In addition no obstacle could be placed in the way of organizing sectarian hierarchal structures or of each religious group's relations with its spiritual leader.[60] As we will see in the next chapter most of this article was, from the Romanian point of view, irrelevant

---

George I. Brătianu, *Origines et formation de l'unité roumaine* (Bucharest: Institut d'Histoire Universelle "N. Iorga," 1943), 253.

[59] *Documente privind istoria României, războiul pentru independență*, IX, 382.

[60] *Aus dem Leben König Karls*, 81.

and/or overkill. Their consistent posture centered on the contention that there had never existed anything resembling religious bigotry in the Danubian Principalities. Rather, from their perspective, the ominously operative portion of Article XLIV came in the specification that everyone in Romania might now enjoy civil and political rights.

Several intriguing insights emerge from an analysis of the background and editing of Article XLIV. If we compare the text of the Serbian with the Romanian sections of the Congress's decrees, we discover that the respective articles on minority rights are identical for the first two paragraphs, but then a third paragraph on the subject appears only in the article affecting the Romanian Jewish community. There the Powers insisted that their nationals, whether merchants or otherwise, must be treated on a basis of perfect equality and without distinction as to religious preference while on Romanian soil.[61] Obviously, as we have seen in the negotiations for the Romanian-German and Romanian-Italian commercial conventions, the Powers had lingering anxieties regarding Romanian compliance and their own economic interests. And nothing they had heard in their month in Berlin gave them reason to believe that this extra stipulation in the Romanian equation was anything but necessary. More significantly for the career of Jewish rights in Romania, Bismarck presented a facade of simply following the humanitarian leads of France and Italy. As it turned out his adamant support of Article XLIV of the Congress of Berlin had at least as much to do with political leverage on the Romanian government as it did with any idealism flowing out of the heritage of the French Revolution. As one Romanian commentator observed, perhaps with as much acerbity as frankness, Bismarck saw in Article XLIV "a means of blackmail" to be used against Bucharest to achieve purposes other than the improvement of Jewish rights such as he had promised Gerson von Bleichröder.[62]

---

[61] For the complete text of the Congress of Berlin's decrees, see *Nouveau recueil général de Traités*, 449–65; to compare the Serbian and Romanian articles, see 460 & 462–3 respectively.

[62] Gh. Cazan, "Recunoașterea internațională a independenței de stat a României," *Reprezentanțele Diplomatice ale României*. I (1859–1917). (București: Editura Politică, 1967), 24; Mite Kremnitz, *Regele Carol I al României*, Const. Graur (trans.), (București: Editura "Universala" Alcalay & Co., 1909), 139.

That Bismarck intended to maneuver behind the cover of the Jewish rights issue first surfaced during the Congress's session of 10 July. In the process of editing the text of their decisions relative to equality of rights and freedom of religion, the delegates sought some common phraseology that would apply to all the countries involved (i.e., Bulgaria, Montenegro, Serbia, and Romania). Even among this diversity the Romanian situation evidenced a special problem in the difficulty of accurately defining the nationality of its Jewish community. In an effort to prevent misunderstanding the Italian ambassador to Berlin, Count de Launay, proposed that the Congress's article on Romania be altered to read "the Jews of Romania, in so much as they do not possess other nationality, will acquire Romanian nationality without further need of certification." This proposal went far beyond the original language adopted by the Congress. It not only undercut the Romanian contention that there were no Romanian Jews, just immigrants from Galicia and Russia, but also conferred upon that community indisputable rights of citizenship. Such an improvement in Article XLIV's specificity, then, would have clearly exposed any Romanian equivocation on minority rights. Furthermore it would have preempted the next eighteen months of diplomatic wangling in which the Romanians attempted to avoid the full effects of the Great Powers' determinations. Unfortunately for the Romanian Jews, Bismarck resorted to obstructionist parliamentary tactics claiming that it would be "inconvenient to have to modify resolutions already adopted by the Congress." More to his point, the proposed Italian revision would have robbed him of the only leverage he possessed in the Romanian railroad issue. Thus, he stressed that the delegates should continue with their editing work on its original basis and without rehashing points already settled. The Congress accepted his point, both on the level of parliamentary procedure and to accommodate the widest possible set of opinions. Once Gorchakov reiterated the Russian dislike of such articles dealing with the Jews in Romania, the whole matter of revisions was dropped.[63]

By mid July of 1878, then, the Romanian government found itself facing the Great Powers over these issues. Even more

---

[63] "Protocole No. 17. Séance du 10 Juillet 1878," *Nouveau recueil général de Traités*, 431.

fundamentally it had to decide whether or not it would accept as authoritative the outcome of the deliberations at Berlin. Prime Minister Brătianu, Foreign Minister Kogălniceanu, and other leading members of the government all advised Prince Carol to endorse fully the articles pertaining to Romania. With Romania's independence at stake, they concurred in counseling the utmost circumspection and that absolutely no display of testiness be permitted. Unluckily for their plans, by this date both houses of the Romanian parliament and the politically aware portion of the population were quite aroused by the projected loss of Bessarabia and the question of Jewish rights. While it might not be feasible to resist the Russian Empire, the Jewish population (particularly the large number of recent Ashkenazic immigrants) posed a different sort of challenge, one which might be ignored or turned aside. That population did, however, represent for these Romanians a paramount danger to their socioeconomic pattern as well as their perception of the essentials of their culture. The price of independence, namely the granting of citizenship to Romanian Jews, seemed exorbitant to many.[64]

---

[64] *Aus dem Leben,* 83; Frederick Kellogg, "The Structure of Romania Nationalism," *Canadian Review of Studies in Nationalism,* 11 (1984): nr. 1: 32.

The Price of Independence

To say that the Romanians reacted bitterly to the decisions of the Congress of Berlin is to be guilty of the grossest understatement. As we have seen, the government's position focused on the necessity of accepting those determinations as unavoidable. Even within this elite stratum of officials and diplomats, however, the initial emotional response displayed considerable intensity. The preference of the Great Powers for the Jewish community's demands in the area of citizenship and equal rights was seen as a counterfeit humanitarianism, one which neglected the equity of the Romanian position. The Romanians excoriated the accent placed on "lofty principles of civilization" to the detriment of their efforts to construct a nationality. From their viewpoint the pursuit of an independent state had at least as good a claim on the sublime as did the pretensions of the Jews. They also considered their aspirations more solidly rooted in tradition and more graced by sustained sacrifice against great odds. The extreme nature of this revulsion emerged in an article written by Mihai Eminescu (1850–1889) more than a year after the close of the Congress of Berlin. Even after the passage of that much time, Romania's preeminent man of letters, also an important political fixture and a vocal anti-Semite, still fulminated against the extraordinarily high price his country was being asked to pay for its independence. Though by far not the most fanatic of contemporary Romanians where bias came into play, he thought that under existing legal conditions the Jewish community had steadily made dangerous inroads into the social and economic well being of the country. And now

Romania, whose social order had already been compromised by an aggravated "American liberalism," was being forced to admit this "foreign element" into its body politic. Should this happen, Eminescu and those for whom he spoke saw their "Latinity" and their future imperiled.[1]

In addition to feeling that their national character was under siege, many influential Romanians also believed that they had been deceived. The most pessimistic among them had expected that the sacrifice of Bessarabia would bring with it the long awaited recognition of Romanian independence by the Great Powers. This loss of territory the Russians had hinted at for some time and then exacted in the period of San Stefano. But these Romanian political leaders had not anticipated fighting a victorious war and then being met with yet another more indiscriminate prerequisite to national self-determination. To understand the Romanian apprehension of the Jewish question, then, we must realize that it combined both the substance of the issue as well as a strong sense of having been victimized in a humiliating fashion. What happened to them as a consequence of the Congress of Berlin the Romanians ardently believed to be completely unwarranted.[2] Similar passions and an accompanying panorama of political forebodings likewise found expression at court.

Prince Carol shared the deep sense of rancor felt by politician and citizen alike over the loss of Bessarabia and the perceived perils of Jewish emancipation, but he clearly saw the potential damage to his position and that of the dynasty. He found himself caught between the resentment of his population and the realization that it would be impossible to resist the will of Europe in these matters. The reports of Romania's diplomatic agents left no doubt in his mind that there would be no recognition of his government's independence until the decrees issued at Berlin were accepted. Prince and government were likewise aware that they had suffered a major public

---

[1] *Independenţa României, Documente*, IV (*Documente Diplomatice, 1873–1881*), A. Gr. Paraipan, A. N. Popescu & C. I. Turco (eds.), (Bucureşti: Editura Academiei Republicii Socialiste Românâ, 1978), 433; M. Eminescu, "Preţul independenţei noastre," *Opera politică*. I (1870–1879), I. Creţu (ed.), (Bucureşti: Cugetarea—Georgescu Delafras, 1941), 518–20.

[2] Titu Maiorescu, *Istoria Contimporană a României (1866–1900)*, (Bucureşti: Editura Librăriei Socec & Co., 1925), 167.

FIGURE IV. Mihai Eminescu. From: *Holidays in Romania, 1989.*

relations setback in the comparison with Serbia. The Romanian envoy in Belgrade reported that the demands made for Jewish equality had simply not generated anything like the level of bitterness nor the public protests so much in evidence in Romania. While embracing the basic Romanian motif that the entire Jewish community possessed only the legal status enjoyed by all other foreigners, Prince Carol determined to carry off the acceptance of the Berlin decisions with honor and in his own best interests. To accomplish this he believed the question of anti-Jewish disabilities would have to be played out through the mechanism of party politics and in the arena of a special legislative session called for constitutional revision.[3] On the diplomatic front Carol and Kogălniceanu from the very beginning of this struggle informed all Romanian emissaries abroad to work for the establishment of full diplomatic relations. Bucharest desired completely accredited ambassadors, nothing less. Mistakenly, the Prince thought he might be able to obtain fully commissioned ministers from the Great Powers and in this fashion gain some ground in the dispute over the Congress's protocols affecting Romania.[4]

Both the Romanian government and court felt compelled to proceed with some urgency as well as circumspection. Prince Karl Anton, Carol's father, wrote to him in late August advising the speediest possible action on the question of Bessarabia. His recommendation to his son centered on the unavoidable loss of that province and the necessity at this time to concentrate on the advantages that the acquisition of the Dobrogea would give the Romanian dynasty. The dictates of the Congress of Berlin should be acquiesced in as those of fate and must not be permitted to create a debilitating condition of estrangement with the Russian Empire. Foreign Minister Kogălniceanu, after conferring with leaders in the West, likewise held the opinion that the Romanian government had to act with dispatch. He believed the Great Powers were watching Romania's handling of the Bessarabian issue to gauge the Bucharest government's willingness to accommodate itself to Europe's will in other matters. Furthermore, Kogălniceanu was convinced that the longer the delay on the question of Jewish equality then the more influence the Alliance Israélite[5] would

---

[3] *Aus dem Leben König Karls von Rumänien: Aufzeichnungen eines Augenzeugen*, IV (Stuttgart: Cotta'sche Buchhandlung, 1900), 86–9 & 92.

[4] *Independenţa României, Documente*, IV, 391–2; *Aus dem Leben*, 92–3.

[5] Founded in Paris in 1860, the Alliance Israélite Universelle had as one of its primary objectives the defense of Jewish liberties throughout Europe. In pursuing this cause in the case of the Romanian Jewish community the Alliance Israélite held conferences in Brussels (1872) and Paris (1875). During the debates of the Congress of Berlin as well as later during the diplomatic wangling preceding Romanian independence, the Alliance interceded repeatedly to protect Jewish civil and religious rights.

gain in the West. He specifically reported that France and Great Britain would wait for a vote on Jewish emancipation before sending ambassadors to Bucharest. Romania would have to engage in the diplomatic forum from a position of inferiority, then, as well as respond to increased pressures on her domestic politics from outside sources. Until some proof of her goodwill and acceptance of the system worked out at the Congress of Berlin should be forthcoming, resident ministers and not fully accredited ambassadors would be the norm.[6] By the beginning of September Carol wanted to start the process through which the cession of Bessarabia to Russia and some adjustment of the position of the Romanian Jewish community would be worked out. Besides the counsel he had received from various sources, he thought it best to act before the Great Powers could think of new burdens to lay on him and his adopted country. Unfortunately, in his anxiety to get on with the task of integrating the newly acquired territories into an independent Romania he underestimated the degree of resistance that would be encountered in the legislature. Though many he talked with seemed to acknowledge the wisdom of placating the concert of Europe and attempting to secure the most for Romania from a nocuous situation, this rational approach would be the exception in the course of the debates over the upcoming months. In this frame of mind Carol had his consuls inform the governments to which they were accredited that, as painful as it might be, his government would conform to the stipulations of the Congress of Berlin. They also reported to the major capitals in the West that the Romanian legislature had been called for 27 September to act on these demands. The special session for the required constitutional revision could, however, only take place once all foreign troops had left Romanian soil.[7]

Between themselves Kogălniceanu and Prince Carol decided that the "Address from the Throne" scheduled for the opening of the special session of the legislature would be read by the foreign minister. They also agreed to hint at the stipulated amelioration of conditions for the Jewish community. Carol's speech,

---

[6] *Aus dem Leben*, 95–7; Marcel Dinu, Octavian Gaurişi & Cornel Paraschiv, "Dezvoltarea relaţiilor internaţionale ale României," *Diplomaţia română în slujba independenţei*, Vasile Gliga et al. (eds.), (Bucureşti: Editura Politică, 1977), 239.

[7] *Aus dem Leben*, 98 & 100.

as would be expected, made great play over the heroic performance of the army in the Ottoman war. He called upon the deputies and senators to demonstrate an exemplary patriotism by doing their part to insure the prompt according of diplomatic recognition by the Western Great Powers. The loss of Bessarabia he made to seem less damaging by emphasizing that the Dobrogea with its increased access to the Black Sea had been obtained. In this vein he likewise stressed that the Russian and Ottoman Empires had already formally recognized Romanian independence. In this speech that runs to three typewritten pages, however, the reader will find but a single sentence dealing with the matter that most perturbed Romanian politics and impeded for months the acquisition of diplomatic relations with the West; namely, the legal disabilities suffered by the Jewish population. Though not mentioned by name, Carol did refer to their situation in calling upon the legislators to respond to Europe's will by deleting from the constitution those provisions mandating inequality based on religious factors. Having already paraded Romanian self-interest in the situation, Carol proclaimed that the present constitution did not correspond with the ethical level of the nineteenth century, for it incorporated this principle of religious intolerance which remained offensive to Europe as a whole.[8] At this point the difference in importance and emotional impact of the two issues, the loss of Bessarabia and the granting of legal equality to the Jewish community, began to emerge. The Romanian Chamber of Deputies and Senate were not, for their part, as susceptible as Carol to the counsel for haste in accepting the decrees of the Congress of Berlin. On 10 and 12 October respectively the Chamber and Senate expressed their reluctantly given consent to the retrocession of Bessarabia. In order to obtain the Dobrogea and not to frustrate the European peace, they would make the painful sacrifice demanded of them in this regard. But they would not act quickly or even address at this time the question of equal rights for the Jews. As unpleasant as the discussion on Bessarabia had been, the Romanian political leaders evinced even more resentment towards what they termed "that other question." They had felt under duress in

---

[8] *Independenta Romaniei, Documente,* IV, 448–51; *Aus dem Leben,* 106–7.

giving up Bessarabia but were not yet willing to be coerced by the Great Powers on the matter of minority rights. As bad as the deprivation of this traditional Romanian territory might be, the problem of full legal equality for the Jews amounted in their minds to a totally dissimilar issue in terms of the magnitude of its impact on their society.[9]

As much as Prince Carol desired the expeditious passage of the legislation required to satisfy the Berlin norms, he quickly learned that the Jewish issue could not be settled promptly or pleasantly. In mid November he wrote rather pessimistically to his father regarding "the great social revolution" that the Congress of Berlin had forced upon Romania. By this stage of the process he also maintained that the Great Powers were making a mistake, one guaranteed only to increase the bitterness felt over the Jewish issue, by trying to force the pace of constitutional adaptation. To some extent Carol shared the anticipation of Romanian political notables that Great Power influence would not hasten the adoption of a more humane stand on minority rights. Indeed, his basal conception of contemporary Romania dwelt on its character as both an economically and politically underdeveloped nation. Obviously more time and a gentler transition would be needed than Jewish advocates abroad would tolerate.[10] The careful handing of the situation deemed requisite by Carol can be seen in his treatment of the new province of Dobrogea as well as in his cultivation of the northeast province of Moldavia where the vast majority of Jewish immigrants from Galicia and Russia[11] resided. In preparation for Carol's entrance into the newly acquired Dobrogea at the end of November 1878 the government broadcast a proclamation assuring each inhabitant of the region the full protection of the Romanian constitution. This decree specifically announced that, whatever the individual's nation-

---

[9] *Aus dem Leben*, 108–11.

[10] Ibid., 129–30.

[11] As we will see in Chapters IV ("The Voice of the Intelligentsia") and V ("The Quality of Our Jews"), Romanian anti-Semites dwelt on what they perceived as qualitative differences between types of Jews at least as much as they did on the simple fact of Jewishness. In the case of the Jews of Galicia and Russia, anti-Semitic rhetoric concentrated on the culture (especially the dress and speech) of the Hasidic community as being alien and objectionable. Present, of course, was an implied, invidious comparison with the more familiar Sephardic community which was deemed to be less inimical to national interests.

ality or religion, the Romanian courts would not deviate from their duty of equal justice for all. Transparently meant for public relations purposes transcending the acquisition of the Dobrogea, this announcement indicating the Court's attempt to balance native resistance to equality for the Jews with foreign diplomatic pressure did not prove effectual. Insistence on altering Article 7 of the constitution could not be so easily undercut.[12]

Moldavia and its determined, even fanatical, opposition to Jewish rights constituted an even greater problem for Carol's government. Throughout the months-long process of negotiating a compromise which would allow at least seeming acceptance of Berlin's dictates on Jewish rights, the Moldavian deputies and senators consistently dodged every binding commitment on the subject. Virtually every regional leader, secular and religious, initially opposed the government's position. Most dramatically, given the rural and Orthodox nature of the region, Carol had to spend hours pleading with the Metropolitan of Iași (Iosif Naniescu). The Prince all but begged the prelate to display some measure of tolerance and not to feed the dangerous prejudices then disturbing the province. Carol had already failed to persuade the secular political leaders with arguments emphasizing the need for objectivity and for acknowledgment of the threats from the outside world. So too he could not now convince the Metropolitan to use his office to preach peace and concord. The clergyman rather belligerently countered that he would not see Christian Moldavia turned over to the Jews. He refused to reconcile himself to Carol's eloquent pleas to show more tolerance than the anti-Semites who then plagued the government's attempts to satisfy the Great Powers. Though Carol would continue to demonstrate his sympathy and political sensitivity by visiting Moldavia, the extremist antagonism persisted until the end. Indeed, as the crucial ballot on minority rights approached, the Metropolitan of Iași threatened to excommunicate any one who dared "to vote for the Jews."[13] The question of Jewish rights and the revision of Article 7 of the Romanian constitution, then, provoked an unheard of disturbance among all elements of the population. Moreover, it attracted into active polit-

---

[12] Ibid., 136
[13] Ibid., 176, 187–8, 196, & 250.

ical life and the world of party strife many who had not engaged in such partisan demonstrations before. Though the Jewish question agitated both provinces, Moldavia displayed a more violent temperament and produced endless petitions militating against alterations in Article 7. The northern province rejected any and all innovations in the status quo for minorities. Carol and his government found themselves under siege trying to placate adversaries with mutually exclusive demands. From the viewpoint of Moldavian traditionalists and of anti-Semites throughout Romania, any effort to open the door to increased Jewish legal and political rights meant the government had acceded to radical demands for modification in the country's social structure. According to the standpoint of the Alliance Israélite and the Great Powers, however, only the most liberal endorsement of what they considered legitimate Jewish rights and civilized opinion on equity for minorities would satisfy the Congress's prescriptions. At home Carol was assailed as pro-Jewish, while abroad his detractors saw him as vacillating in his support of equality for that community.[14] Meeting these contrary goals and attaining the status of a duly recognized sovereign state, therefore, would necessitate some considerable finesse in the areas of public relations and legal niceties.

In order to gauge the nature of this conflict as well as the manner of its resolution, we must look further at Article 16 of the Civil Code of 1864 and the constitutional adjustment of 1866. The Romanian tradition vis-à-vis its Jewish population involved a complex of Kafkaesque bureaucratic impediments infused with an emotional prejudice of some virulence. As a result of the Convention of Paris (1858) the Romanian Principalities received a mandate from the Great Powers to permit the exercise of political rights independent of religious considerations. Article 46 of that Convention introduced into the Romanian legal structure a measure of progress and moderation vastly superior to that contained in the previous constitutional framework (i.e., the *Règlement Organique* of each province). The anti-Jewish prejudices that had been enshrined in law now had to be altered somewhat, if only on paper.[15] The

---

[14] Ibid., 199–200, 205, & 225.

[15] I. Ionașcu, P. Bărbulescu, & Gh. Sheergha (eds.), *Tratele internaționale ale Româ-niei, 1354–1920* (București: Editura Științifică și Enciclopedică, 1975), 166–7; Joseph Berkowitz, *La Question des Israélites en Roumanie* (Paris: Jouve et Cie, 1923), 285–6 &

Civil Code of 1864 which flowed from this stipulation of the Paris Convention theoretically accorded the Jews, in the Romanian view, gradual access to political rights. The Jewish community welcomed this alteration as a marked improvement in their lot, although as noted in the last chapter it did not lead to the granting of Romanian citizenship to a single member of the Jewish community. Article 16 of the Civil Code laid out with great specificity the various bureaucratic hurdles that had to be overcome to obtain naturalization. To receive the legal status of a Romanian citizen each individual had to submit a request to the prince detailing: (1) the amount of capital he possessed; (2) his profession; (3) the trade he wished to pursue; and (4) his intention to make his home in Romania. If after ten years residency on Romanian soil he had proven by his manner of life and the work he had performed that he offered some advantage to the state, then he might be naturalized. However this final step could only be taken on the initiative of the ruler. Acting with the consent of the Council of State, the prince had to ask the assembly to pass a decree of naturalization. Once the sovereign signed and promulgated the bill, citizenship was finally awarded. The sole way to bypass the decade long residency requirement was to have the authorities judge that the individual had rendered a signal service to the state. More specifically, such a candidate must have offered a unique talent (or invention) to his adopted country or established a major commercial-industrial enterprise in the Principalities. Even though hedged about with a plethora of technical restrictions, Article 16 still represented a monumental step forward in the status of Romania's Jewish population. Here, for the first time, political rights were to be dispensed without an overt reference to the applicant's sectarian affiliation. Any foreigner, in this abstract, had the right to apply for naturalization.[16] Article 16, if actually applied to the condition of the Jewish community, represented a decisive and liberal modification. By contemporary Romanian standards, this vicissitude

---

292; *Constitution des israélites d'après le Règlement organique de la principauté de Moldavie* in Isidore Loeb, *La Situation des Israélites en Turquie, en Serbie et en Roumanie* (Paris: Joseph Baer et Cie, 1877), 197–8.

[16] Constantin C. Giurescu, *Viața și opera lui Cuza Vodă* (București: Editura Științifică, 1966), 311–12; Berkowitz, *La Question des Israélites en Roumanie*, 288 & 292; *Convention de Paris du 7/10 avril 1858* in Loeb, *La Situation de Israélites*, 201.

had the potential to affect the social and economic systems as well as the political.

At this stage we should point out that, when the constitutional crises of 1878–1879 finally wound down, the Romanian legislature manipulated the Jewish question very much in the spirit of the Civil Code of 1864. But this type of brief survey of Romanian legal precepts was not what attracted the attention of the Great Powers in 1878. Rather they manifested significant concern over the Constitution of 1866 which in Article 7 did away with all the pretense we have just scrutinized. It baldly stated that only foreigners belonging to a Christian sect could aspire to Romanian citizenship. Furthermore, it incorporated into the state's constitutional framework an amorphous prescription that citizenship could be acquired or lost according to legislative discretion. At the Congress of Berlin, then, a combination of blatant bias and a legally encoded attitude portending arbitrary actions drew attention to Romania's constitution. Ultimately the historical pattern of bureaucratic obstacles preventing the actual enjoyment of rights promised minorities such as Jews remained unknown (or, perhaps simply ignored). Moreover, an additional determinative factor overlooked throughout this period was the notion that the prospective citizen had to be "useful" ("*utile*") to the state. This aptitude for service formed an essential part of the anti-Semitic doctrine elaborated by the Romanian intelligentsia before World War I. Whether we look at the *Règlement Organique* for either Moldavia or Wallachia, the Civil Code of 1864, or the revised constitution of 1879, every foreigner (Christian or Jew) had to demonstrate that it would benefit Romania for him to be granted citizenship. While quite obviously presenting extensive opportunities for subjectivity and evasion, this emphasis on utility to the state likewise gave an outré cast to Romanian nationalism as well as to its omnipresent corollary of anti-Semitism. This singularity with its stress on usefulness to the nation would help communicate to Romanian anti-Semitism its character of being fortuitously providential.[17]

As the Romanian parliament opened its extraordinary session in late November of 1878, there ensued the greatest con-

---

[17] Frédéric Damé, *Histoire de la Roumanie Contemporaine* (Paris: Germer Baillière et Cie, 1900), 425–6; Loeb, *La Situation des Israélites*, 201–2 & 205–7.

stitutional debate in that nation's history. Both the public and
the legislators engaged in a frequently violent discussion until
the final passage on 25 October 1879 of a revision purported
to satisfy the requirements of the Congress of Berlin. The
Chamber of Deputies and the Senate, backed by widespread
popular indignation, intended to resist complying with the
Great Powers' wishes. The Moldavians in particular cited a
determination not to become a minority in their own homeland. Having already suffered what they considered a mass
invasion by Russian and Galician Jews who now dominated[18]
their economy, they adamantly rejected any constitutional alteration that might lead to a similar colonial status on the political level. One of the inconsistencies in Romania's nationalism
manifested itself here in a mixed attitude towards immigration.
While recognizing that the social level of the country remained
such that some influx of economically capable individuals had
to be allowed, they could not tolerate that indispensable talent
coming from a people so different from themselves.[19] The
Romanians' sense of being aggrieved and agitated over the
Jewish question increased due to their somewhat cynical interpretation of the Great Powers' motivation. As voiced by Foreign Minister Kogălniceanu in the months just before the parliament met to consider the prerequisites for independence,
the delegates at the Congress of Berlin were not primarily inter-
ested in Romanian Jews. Rather they demonstrated more regard
for the mere acceptance of the principle of political and civil
equality. While this interference in Romania's domestic affairs

---

[18] Throughout the eighteenth, nineteenth, and much of the twentieth centuries
Romanian society depended on other ethnic groups to provide the services associated with a middle class. The Armenian and Greek merchants along with those from
the Jewish community fulfilled the tasks normally carried out by a national, urban
middle class. In doing so they earned the enmity of the Romanian nationalist. In
the nineteenth century, the growing Jewish population gained a significant position
as small merchants and wholesale dealers. With the Romanians divided almost exclusively into an exploited peasantry and the aristocracy, the Jews supplied the talent
and entrepreneurship that would otherwise have been lacking to the country. The
nationalistic anti-Semite, though on occasion recognizing the indispensable economic
contribution made by the Jews, still railed at them for supposedly supplanting Romanians (and this despite the fact that Romanians with the same skills, education, and/or
motivations were not to be found).

[19] Barbu B. Berceanu, "Modificarea, din 1879, a articolului 7 din Constituție," *Studii
și materiale de istorie modernă*, VI (1979), 68; Damé, *Histoire de la Roumanie Contemporaine*,
319–20; Șerban Rădulescu-Zoner, "Poziția internațională a României dupa Congresul
de la Berlin. Premise de unei opțiuni," *Studii și materiale de Istorie Modernă*, VI (1979), 48.

seemed for the moment to be a crass infringement of the nation's sovereignty, to Kogălniceanu's mind his country had but to make a bow in the direction of French revolutionary sentiments to reap the benefits of the Congress; namely, independence and the Dobrogea. Since Europe erroneously considered the Jews a part of the homeland, they should swallow their pride and proceed to resolve the matter in conformity with the fundamental interests of Romanian society. Kogălniceanu at this juncture hinted at what would be the way out for the parliament, the use of categories to determine which individuals could be naturalized. Once the mechanism of categorization was embraced, the possibility of limiting access to citizenship could be pursued regardless of any imposed facade of religious tolerance and equality of rights.[20]

When Prince Carol addressed the new legislative session on 27 November, he chose to take an extremely positive tack emphasizing all the good things that had transpired recently. Russia and the Porte now recognized Romania's independence. The country officially belonged to the family of European nations and had acquired the Dobrogea. On this basis he appealed to the patriotism of the legislators, asking them to summon a constituent assembly to abolish political inequality based on religious factors. They had to accept that anti-Semitic disabilities poorly corresponded with the values of the nineteenth century. As we would expect, however, the political leadership in the parliament responded by spending the time between November 1878 and the opening of the constitutional revision assembly on 3 June 1879 engaged in partisan political struggles. Unable to rise to Prince Carol's exhortation they simply reflected the enormous anti-Jewish agitation present in the country. Indeed, Carol would find through the remainder of 1878 and almost to the conclusion of the constitutional debates in 1879 virtually no one among the political elite who was willing to heed his message. Regardless of party affiliation the politically prominent stood shoulder to shoulder in opposing a liberal proposition of this magnitude.[21] Instead these deputies

---

[20] Mihail Kogălniceanu, *Opere*, IV, Georgeta Penelea (ed.), (Bucureşti: Editura Academiei Republicii Socialiste Românía, 1978), 622 & 637–41.

[21] Carol Iancu, *Les Juifs en Roumanie (1866–1919) de l'Exclusion a l'Emancipation* (Aix-en-Provence: Editions de l'Université de Provence, 1978), 168. *Aus dem Leben*, 141, 157, & 220.

and senators were fixated on the popular animosity generated
by the presence of hundreds of thousands of Russian and Galician Jews concentrated in Moldavia. Adding to this tension
and to their apprehension over national cohesiveness was the
perception that Jewish immigration into Romanian territories
had accelerated in the last two decades.[22] The contemporary
reasoned defense for the presence of Article 7 in the Romanian
constitution centered, therefore, on the necessity of preventing
further migration of "Polish" Jews into Romania. This rationalization continued on to maintain that the prohibition against
nonChristians becoming Romanian citizens had nothing to do
with religion. Since tolerance had supposedly been a trade-
mark of the Danubian Principalities for centuries, Romanian
anti-Semites adamantly refused to concede any lapses on the
score of sectarian prejudice. Cutting across social lines there
arose a sentiment opposed to further concessions. Having made
the sacrifice of Bessarabia the conservative element in Romania
proclaimed that it would not countenance a constitutional revision likely to bring on a "social revolution."[23]

In an attempt to bridge the gap to the conservative forces
and at the same time conciliate the champions of Jewish rights
outside Romania, Carol chose to emphasize the socioeconomic
nature of the problem. By doing so he hoped to induce the
circumspection required to deal successfully with so sensitive
an issue. He especially wished to convey to the Germans some
sense of the political difficulties inherent in meeting the
Congress's demands and of the impossibility of resolving the
predicament with any alacrity. At the opening of the constitutional revision assembly on 3 June 1879, then, Prince Carol

---

[22] Romanian population statistics for the nineteenth century stressed the growth
and concentration of the Jewish community, particularly in Moldavia. In doing so
they followed contemporary nationalistic cant lumping recent immigrants together
with Jewish families resident in the Principalities for generations. Thus, the Jewish
portion of the population of Iași was given as 36 percent in 1831 and 47 percent in
1859. Likewise these population charts adduced the presence of Jews in the mercantile ranks of Iași as 43 percent in 1831, 73 percent in 1846, and 78 percent in 1860. Whatever the accuracy of these statistics, Romanian anti-Semites clearly believed them.
Furthermore, they sounded their anti-Jewish tocsin predicating in the future a similar
or even aggravated growth curve. See Verax [Radu Rosetti], *La Roumanie et les Juifs*
(Bucarest: I. V. Socecu, 1903), 19, 33, & 107.

[23] Mihail Kogălniceanu, *Opere*, V (București: Editura Academiei Republicii Socialiste România, 1984), 9; C. A. Rosetti, *C. A. Rosetti, Gînditorul. Omul*, Radu Pantazi
(ed.), (București: Editura Politică, 1969), 312; R. W. Seton-Watson, *A History of the
Roumanians* (Hamden: Archon Books, 1963), 346–7.

echoed the conservative thesis that Article 7 appeared in the constitution only because of concerns relating to the nation's social structure. Romania having always been a forbearing country, the sole intent of that article had been to impede unrestricted immigration which just happened to be Jewish. He urged the delegates in the best interest of their nation's domestic and international well being to bring the matter to a speedy resolution.[24] After devoting almost his entire speech to this subject, Carol concluded with the observation that, once the delegates removed Article 7's cult-based restrictions on citizenship, they would have satisfied the Great Powers' preoccupation with the Jews. He went out of his way to stress that the principle alone mattered in terms of diplomatic relations and their effect on Romania's vested interests. He shared his conviction with the constituent assembly that the Great Powers neither wanted to nor could regulate the prosecution of the Jewish question in any detail. They certainly would not be in a position "to impose absolute solutions contrary to our most vital interests." By the fall the Romanian government seemed to be receiving subtle indications that Carol's judgments in this regard were quite to the point. The Romanian diplomatic agent in Berlin reported that Chancellor Bismarck had observed that the Jewish question had a long history in the Principalities, one marked by repeated promises to rectify the situation which never came to fruition. Although coupled with the notice that Europe expected something more on this occasion, the fact that the Germans acknowledged previous Romanian equivocation seemed to signal that similar tactics might work again. This impression gained all the more currency, since as early as July Romanian diplomats had reported from Berlin that the Great Powers merely awaited a demonstration of good faith. If Romania would remove Article 7 and then appear to initiate a sincere effort ("*ein loyaler Anfang*") to implement religious equality, the impasse would be resolved. Symbolic acceptance of the principle of religious equality became the unstated minimum, rather than substantive change in the status of the Jewish community.[25]

---

[24] *Aus dem Leben*, 180 & 203.

[25] Iancu, *Les Juifs en Roumanie*, 166; *Independenţa României, Documente*, IV, 419; *Aus dem Leben*, 220.

Eventually this tactic prevailed. As early as the spring of 1879 it had been suggested that Article 7 be removed. This realized, the constitution could then be altered to reflect the same type of impediments to naturalization that had been included in the Civil Code of 1864. Article 44 of the Congress of Berlin only mandated the elimination of what the Great Powers saw as offensive language. Since it did not further intrude into the domestic legislation of the country, the Romanians could then regulate the matter as they saw fit.[26] But before that stage could be attained, the Romanian constitutional revision assembly had to spend months discharging its emotional load. The political volatility of the situation had to work itself out with endless statements of the conservatives' traditional position. Only when this had been accomplished, could the government move on to finesse the situation. Thus, at the beginning of the revision project in July the assembly stated that "There are no Romanian Jews and never have been. . . ." It went on to insist that the Jews in Romania differed in language and customs from the natives and did not have any desire to assimilate. The assembly had as its original intention to authorize the naturalization of any foreigner regardless of his faith, but only on an individual by individual basis. Each grant of citizenship would necessitate special legislation for its legal sanction. This original project presented for discussion by the initiating commission to the assembly prescribed that the procedures for naturalization would also be written into the constitution. At its conclusion, this proposal stipulated that the privilege of owning real property remained a political right and not one of citizenship. The final jab indicated both Romania's continuing reluctance to embrace wholeheartedly the ordinances of Berlin as well as the socioeconomic tensions present. If forced to offer even the possibility of citizenship to the Jewish community, the Romanian conservatives still wanted to withhold any economic advantage that might flow from that status.[27]

This truculence did not help the Romanian cause. Although Bismarck and the Germans would eventually have a hidden agenda to present to the Romanians, throughout this process they insisted on at least a superficial adherence to the dispo-

---

[26] *Aus dem Leben*, 197.
[27] Kogălniceanu, *Opere*, V, 12; *Aus dem Leben*, 214.

sitions arrived at by the Congress of Berlin. Even before the constituent assembly opened Bismarck had expressed his discontent with the nature of Bucharest's parliamentary debates and the blatantly anti-Semitic tone of the Romanian press. These characteristics, of course, continued for the duration of the diplomatic struggle. They perpetuated suspicions that Romania intended to avoid her responsibilities and the full discharge of the Congress's design. Moreover, the extremely limited scope of the initial Romanian proposal vastly misjudged what the more liberal Western Great Powers desired. The French and English wanted Article 44 of the Congress of Berlin interpreted in such a way as to mandate the naturalization of tens of thousands of members of the Romanian Jewish community. Specifically, during the summer of 1879, they advised the Romanian government that its new constitution should specify that any adult born there and not possessing foreign citizenship should be deemed to enjoy all political and civil rights. This suggestion not only exceeded anything remotely considered by the Romanians, but caused turmoil among those who heard of it. If enacted, such a constitutional proviso would incorporate a minimum of one hundred thousand Jews into the electorate. Inconceivably encompassing by the Romanian standard, no constitutional revision assembly could possibly accept such an idea. But the French and English position did indicate to them how great a discrepancy existed between their respective positions as well as the need for some compromise.[28]

Those Romanians who wished to listen already grasped the inadequacy of this original measure for Jewish rights. Even before the assembly opened, the German and Italian governments had brought home to them this objectionable fact in yet another fashion. Bismarck in a most determined manner and the Italian foreign ministry more sotto voce pointed out the contrast between Romanian and Serbian methodologies. Serbia received formal diplomatic recognition of her independence in the spring of 1879. At that point Romania had yet to convene her constitutional assembly for the purpose of revising Article 7's religiously intolerant language. The South Slav state acted promptly and in an appealingly forthright way

---

[28] *Aus dem Leben*, 185, 244, & 248.

to perform as the Great Powers desired. The Danubian Principalities fulminated presenting the distinct impression to even her most ardent advocates (the Italians) of devising subterfuges. Though explicable in terms of historical development and the relative sizes of the two Jewish communities, this comparison represented at the minimum a major public relations gaffe for the Romanians. It certainly meant additional diplomatic pressures for improved constitutional verbiage as a precondition for independence.[29] Another factor overlooked or underestimated initially was the impact of the Jewish lobby in the West, especially in Germany and Italy. Traditional Romanian artifice would surface later, but at the start of the revision debate Bucharest's pugnacity captured more attention than did its finesse. Already aware of Romania's special brand of anti-Semitism, West European Jews determined to use this opportunity to force through real reforms. By appealing to widely acknowledged notions of broadmindedness and civilized behavior, they easily made their case by highlighting the diatribes in the Romanian legislature and press. As long as Romania still awaited the granting of formal recognition by the Great Powers, the possibility of coercing significant change in her treatment of the Jewish population remained. Once fully sovereign in the eyes of the Western Great Powers, however, all leverage pertaining to her domestic affairs would evaporate.[30]

As had been their consistent diplomatic usage since well before the outbreak of the 1877–1878 war, the Romanians continued to maintain a public policy of repulsing all efforts to interfere in their domestic affairs. They refused any country the right to influence policies essential to the nation's well being, and they betrayed an increasing irritability with such meddling. In defending their interests the Romanians habitually asserted that the Jewish question could only be resolved by Romanians and only in a gradual fashion. These arguments emphasized that outside pressures offended Romanian national pride, incited popular opposition, and rendered more difficult than

---

[29] Raoul V. Bossy, *Politica externă a României între anii 1873–1880 privită dela Agenția diplomatică din Roma* (București: Cultura Națională, 1928), 189–90; W. N. Medlicott, "The Recognition of Roumanian Independence, 1878–1880," *Slavonic Review*, 11 (1933), nr. 32: 576–7.

[30] Fritz Stern, *Gold and Iron. Bismarck, Bleichröder, and the Building of the German Empire* (New York: Vintage Books, 1979), 355, 369, & 273.

ever a solution to this quandary. The Romanians ultimately tried to counteract this bad press with a propaganda offensive of their own. Bucharest's foreign office made available to foreign governments and the Western press what it termed "precise information." With this media contrivance it hoped to fend off any deleterious impact of the foreign liberal lobby. While claiming that the charges of religious intolerance were unjust, the government refused to concede anything more than that the 1866 constitution had been "maladroit." At the same time it also insinuated that the turmoil caused by the Jews made them enemies of Romania.[31] Such tactics and self-serving attestations did not satisfy either the proponents of Jewish rights or the Great Powers.

By the late summer and early fall of 1879 the Romanian legislative leadership gradually came to the realization that some diminution of its anti-Jewish rhetoric would be necessary. These men likewise agreed that an appearance of compromise was in order. Kogălniceanu stressed to the delegates that they had to act, even if they considered the Congress of Berlin and its accompanying interference in their affairs a national humiliation. Either the parliament would rewrite the constitution as best it could to protect Romania's interests and existing social order or Europe would take matters into its hands. The foreign minister left no doubt that this could possibly be to the detriment of what the delegates thought proper for their country. There simply did not exist a way to avoid acting within the confines of Article 44 of the Congress of Berlin. The principle of religious tolerance and equal rights for the Jews had to be accepted. To hesitate any longer placed the Romanian nation's vital affairs at risk.[32] The opening to a potential compromise began, then, with the Romanian judgment that the major foreign capitals so insistent on the matter of Article 7 could be placated first by acknowledging the principle involved and second by authorizing a significant number of naturalizations. Either categories of Jews or lists of individuals to be naturalized would probably suffice. The Romanian diplomatic agent

---

[31] Petre Bărbulescu (ed.), *Reprezentanţele diplomatice ale României*, I (Bucureşti: Editura Politică, 1967), 43; Bossy, *Politica externă a României*, 15–6; Damé, *Histoire de la Roumanie Contemporaine*, 318.

[32] Mihail Kogălniceanu, *Opere*, V, 134–6 & 145–6.

in Berlin had already reported that the Germans would be satisfied with certain types of Jews being given citizenship immediately; namely, those who had served in the army, obtained a Romanian secondary diploma or other academic degree, graduated from a foreign university, contributed to the state economically or culturally, and finally anyone who had established a major commercial/industrial enterprise in the country.[33] Once these specifications were satisfied the Jewish question could be put aside. Unfortunately from Bucharest's point of view, the French proved somewhat more difficult to satisfy, at least on paper. Waddington, the foreign minister, informed Bucharest that naturalizations conceded on an individual by individual basis would not be acceptable. Such governmental lists potentially lent themselves to too great a degree of manipulation. Rather France had to insist on categories, whatever they might be and no matter how narrowly defined. Any classification would do as long as it augured compliance with Article 44 and its theoretical underpinnings. The Romanians, therefore, perceived their best polity to be a reversion to the restrictive conditions of 1864. The customary methods of handling the Jewish question in the Principalities might succeed once more. In revising the constitution the assembly had to prepare not only a statement designed to placate the Great Powers, but also one that would detail categories similar to those inserted in the Civil Code of 1864. In this fashion, foreign pressure would be removed, independence garnered, and with some luck the traditional Romanian social order preserved.[34]

With this background of widespread domestic unrest caused by the discussion over Article 7 and the diplomatic imbroglio, the Romanian leadership moved in the direction of accommodation. Their foreign policy apprehensions also intensified due to the country's exposed position relative to the obviously expansionist ambitions of the Russian and Habsburg empires. Whatever the wording, the essence of the compromise from their point of view would consist in doing the minimum required to obtain recognition of Romanian independence, but

---

[33] *Aus dem Leben*, 231–2 & 240.

[34] "Correspondence relative to the Recognition of the Independence of Roumania – 1879–1880," *British and Foreign State Papers*, 71(1879–1880), (London: William Ridgway, 1887), 1163. Kogălniceanu, *Opere*, V, 147.

they proposed to do this without adopting the Great Powers' interpretation of Article XLIV. Or, as formulated by one of the most articulate and important of contemporary Romanian anti-Semites, the Congress of Berlin had espoused its position on equality of rights and religious toleration as a matter of principle. Romania received it in the same vein and voted to remove Article 7 from the constitution *"in principle"* (emphasis in the original). The working out of the technicalities of that removal "in principle" ultimately made the crucial difference, since the two sides had such divergent motivations and goals.[35] How asymmetric the two approaches were even on the eve of compromise can be seen from the first counterproposal of the Romanian opposition. It reluctantly appraised the need for some type of concession on the issue of Article 7. But, then, the opposition's leadership demanded that the insertion of religious equality into the constitution be balanced by a number of conditions for naturalization; namely, that each bill granting citizenship be passed by a two-thirds majority of the Chamber of Deputies and that no lists or categories be employed. Naturalization would be offered to Romania's hundreds of thousands of Jews only on a person by person basis validated by a special act of the legislature. Cumbersome at best, the process obviously intended that there should not be the slightest chance of a successful enforcement in most instances.[36]

In the course of the debates in the constituent assembly in September and early October of 1879, the opposition leaders gradually edged towards relative moderation in their wording of Article 7. However, they still did not embrace the government's more liberal position. Continuing to include the various bureaucratic impediments to naturalization in all its proposals, the assembly placed primary emphasis on its estimate of the country's mood. It also stressed the general support for these obstacles to naturalization on the part of the Romanian people. The government had to understand that no more could be done for the Jews than was being proposed. If more should be attempted, the opposition predicted that the endeavor would guarantee electoral disaster for the government

---

[35] Rădulescu-Zoner, "Poziția internațională a României," 47–9; Rosetti, *C. A. Rosetti, Gînditorul. Omul,* 312.

[36] *Aus dem Leben,* 254.

and its supporters.[37] The attitude towards concessions that
eventually prevailed focused on a formalistic satisfaction of the
demands of the Congress of Berlin. Even then the extreme
anti-Semites accused the proponents of compromise of being
"friends of the Jews." This attitude reflected Romania's increased
strength which brought with it an enhanced ability to maneuver
between the Great Powers. From the anti-Semitic delegates'
point of view this would enable the country to place its own
interpretation on constitutional revision, rather than meekly
subscribing to that of the Congress. They blended the judgment that it now made good sense to give in to Europe's wishes
in this regard with a increasingly sophisticated anti-Semitic
rationalization. Their debates consequently proceeded to analyze how best to use this facade of compliance to protect
Romanian national affairs. Especially interesting at this stage
was the rhetoric employed repeatedly by Titu Maiorescu, one
of the intellectuals turned politician whom we will look at in
the chapter on anti-Semitic ideology. He stressed that the constituent assembly had simply to proclaim that the Congress
of Berlin's dispositions had been satisfied. Such an unembel-
lished declaration would accomplish everything the delegates
desired. With the language of Article 7 of the constitution altered, no Great Power would bother to enter into the web of
Romania's domestic legislation to pursue the matter any further.
Having given lip service to the dictates of Berlin, Romania would
then be in a position to maintain that all subsequent interpre-
tations of the matter concerned only Romanians. According
to Maiorescu no challenge to Europe would be necessary. Rather
the delegates would have the law on their side in any further
discussion of minority rights. Since they would have met the
requirements of Berlin, they could then maintain their right
to decide issues directly affecting Romania's self-interest. But
most importantly Maiorescu illustrated that the conservation
of the Romanian nationality could remain, both before and
after this pro forma acquiescence, the prime consideration.[38]

The government and constituent assembly, then, proceeded
in a manner exceptionally reminiscent of the tone as well as

---

[37] Titu Maiorescu, *Discursuri parlamentare*, II(1876–1881). (Bucureşti: Editura Lib-
rǎriei Socecŭ & Comp., 1897), 313, 324–6, & 329–30.

[38] Ibid., 341 & 362–6.

FIGURE V. Titu Maiorescu. From: *Titu Maiorescu*, Editura Pentru Literatură, 1967.

the specifics of the Civil Code of 1864. The compromise they worked out revised Article 7 of the Romanian constitution so as to remove the blatantly anti-Semitic character of the 1866 version. The emendation duly proclaimed that confessional differences did not constitute an impediment to the acquisition or exercise of political and religious rights in Romania. Article 7 now specifically stated that any foreigner not a citizen of another state or under its protection could be naturalized, but this opportunity would only be forthcoming if the non-Romanian met certain conditions. Once more the petitioner for Romanian citizenship had to satisfy the government's Levantine procedures for naturalization. Intended to insure that the process would be as tortuous as possible, these proceedings included a statement on the applicant's finances, profession, and place of abode in the country. Again as in the 1860s the candidate for citizenship had to satisfy a residency requirement of ten years and prove by his actions that he was a useful inhabitant. Exempted from these preconditions were those who contributed an especially useful invention or talent, established major commercial enterprises, or otherwise significantly assisted the economy. In addition, children born in Romania to resident aliens, educated there, and likewise never subjects of a foreign power might also bypass the more usual conditions for naturalization. Finally, the one category for which this whole process would make a substantial difference, all those who had served in the Romanian war of independence would be naturalized collectively and without any added formalities on the government's part. In contrast to the soldiers of the 1877–1878 war with the Ottoman Empire, all other cases for naturalization had to be treated separately and confirmed individually by the legislature. The revised Article 7 went on to specify that the Romanian Chamber and Senate had to pass a special law determining how a foreigner might establish his domicile in the country. Only Romanian citizens (born or naturalized) could own rural properties. And the new article reiterated that all existing rights possessed by individuals or countries by virtue of international conventions remained in force.[39]

Although equality of rights and the prospect of immediate naturalization for most of the Jewish community would obviously remain remote under this revision, the extremist opposition did not abate, but, despite an impassioned anti-Jewish speech on the part of one of Romania's outstanding men of letters, the compromise did survive. In the Chamber of Deputies the vote tally was one hundred thirty-three for the revision with nine opposing. In the Senate the outcome was fifty-six to two. Prince Carol promulgated the newly revised article of the constitution on 24 October 1879. By that date, then, the Romanians saw themselves as having given the West a major concession at the possible expense of their social order. The Great Powers, however, were not so easily placated.[40] However much the Romanians thought they had sacrificed and com-

[39] *Aus dem Leben*, 254–5; Damé, *Histoire de la Roumanie Contemporaine*, 426.
[40] *Aus dem Leben*, 256.

promised in bringing forth this revised version of Article 7, the outside world did not share their opinion. The Great Powers and the other Western advocates of Jewish rights had a decidedly bad impression of this constitutional change and the atmosphere out of which it sprang. This impression was reinforced within a week of the passage of the constitutional reform by the announcement of the administrative procedures to be employed in the naturalization of Romanian Jews. The British minister to Bucharest, William White, reported to the Foreign Office on the Kafkaesque paperwork requirements. Ignoring the unsettled recent history of the area and the conflict of interest on the part of the Romanian bureaucracy, each applicant for naturalization had to produce: (a) a registration of birth; (b) his identity card; (c) testimonials as to his usefulness to the country; (d) proof of his parents' residency in Romania; (e) an affidavit proving that neither he nor his parents had ever enjoyed the protection of a foreign government; (f) a certificate demonstrating that he had not attempted to avoid the draft by claiming foreign allegiance; and (g) a warrant evidencing the renunciation of foreign protection if ever possessed. Given this area of Europe's well deserved reputation for bureaucratic harassment, the Great Powers' suspicions as to what the Romanians envisaged were well taken. Indeed, grave doubts would exist as to the producibility of these items, even if all of them had ever existed. Western perceptions, therefore, centered on the less than generous espousal of equality of rights by the Romanian government. Anticipating such a reaction, Bucharest had already directed its agents abroad to take the line that the restrictions incorporated into the revised edition of Article 7 represented a relatively unimportant portion of the legislation. They were simply a codicil that acknowledged the all too real nationalistic movement in the country. This upsurge of chauvinist fervor could neither be ignored nor stemmed, just channeled. The cool reception received by its constitutional labors also compelled Bucharest to begin considering immediate naturalization en bloc of a number of Jews to establish its good intentions.[41]

With the ostensible fulfillment of Article XLIV of Berlin out of the way, the Romanian government still faced a prolonged

---

[41] "Correspondence relative to the Recognition of the Independence of Roumania," *British and Foreign State Papers*, 1178; *Aus dem Leben*, 256–7.

process of diplomatic bargaining in order to obtain its recognition as an independent state. Italy indicated her willingness to proceed with formal recognition, but could not act until the other three Western Great Powers did so. England wanted the naturalization of at least a few members of the Jewish community, while France desired that much and more. Germany, the key to the situation, continued to manipulate the naturalization issue. Bismarck, however, did so now on a practical rather than a humanitarian plane so as to pursue more efficaciously economic interests (a solution to troubled German investment in Romania's railroads). The Romanians persisted in brandishing the tendentious defense that the vast majority of the Jewish community were unassimilated recent immigrants. They also maintained that these migrants enjoyed an improved status in Romania. At this point they set out to prove their sincerity and the integrity of the new equal rights article, and the granting of citizenship to a manageable number of Jews would undercut the calumnies carried in the foreign press about Romania's treatment of religious minorities.[42] The government returned, then, to a plan discussed in Romanian diplomatic circles earlier in the year. It announced to the Great Powers its determination to proceed directly to the naturalization of "all the Jews, who are Romanian subjects, that we find assimilated." As limited as this statement of purpose was, it did not detail the complete blueprint to authenticate Romanian generosity and good will, for the manifest intent, from the very inception of the idea, centered on bestowing citizenship only on a small number of veterans. Remembering the pervasive hostility to the Jews and this whole issue, we will not be surprised to discover that the assembly originally devised a project encompassing a grand total of one thousand seventy-five potential new citizens. Of these approximately four-fifths came from the ranks of veterans who had fought in the war for independence. In the end the result of this exercise would be even fewer new Jewish citizens then envisioned in this severely circumscribed scheme.[43]

The tenor of the debates and the motives involved perhaps best manifested themselves in the observations of Kogălniceanu.

---

[42] Stern, *Gold and Iron*, 352–4; *Aus dem Leben*, 167 & 211; Bossy, *Politica externă a României*, 14–5.

[43] *Independența României, Documente*, IV, 465; Berkowitz, *La Question des Israélites en Roumanie*, 651; Iancu, *Les Juifs en Roumanie*, 168.

He helped persuade the assembly by saying he was convinced these Jews would be good citizens. He felt this way because, if they did not pass muster, their coreligionists would be so much the worse off, and, perhaps, the doorway to citizenship would close tight for a considerable time. Besides, five hundred or a thousand Jewish citizens would not endanger Romania. On 24 and 25 October the Chamber and Senate passed the mass naturalization bill by approximately the same margins as they had the theoretical statement on equality of rights in Article 7. Most legislators voted for it even if reluctantly, with a few nays and abstentions from the truly rabid anti-Semites. In hindsight Kogălniceanu's estimate that this limited enfranchisement of Jewish veterans portended no harm to the state or to the assembly's nationalistic objectives served as a less than subtle cue that there need be few more such naturalizations. Resulting from this ballot some eight hundred and eighty-eight Jewish veterans received Romanian citizenship. Unfortunately, from the perspective of the Great Powers and of Jewish rights advocates, no new ground was broken here. This naturalization en masse stood out as neither a legal innovation nor an auspicious precedent. It simply awarded civil and political rights to individuals who would mostly have been eligible under the guidelines of the Civil Code of 1864. Parading the government's loyal application of the decisions made at Berlin, rather than executing substantive change, remained Kogălniceanu's and the assembly's primary purpose.[44]

Since we have looked in some detail at the political process by which Romania worked out the mandate to grant equality to her Jews, we must now turn to analyze the interplay of Romanian domestic concerns with the aims of the Great Powers. For Bucharest had not only failed to accomplish all that the Berlin decisions seemed to require, but had also lacked the capacity to display from the beginning the exemplary public image that its diplomatic agent in Berlin had insisted was so crucial. This same intermediary subsequently reported that the Western Great Powers had pledged to maintain a common front where the fulfillment of the Congress's resolutions was involved.[45] But by late 1879 Romanian self-interest and her

---

[44] Kogălniceanu, *Opere*, V, 179 & 181–2; *Aus dem Leben*, 257.
[45] Nichita Adăniloaie, "Berlin," *Reprezentanţele Diplomatice ale României*, I (1859–1917). (Bucureşti: Editura Politică, 1967), 232; *Aus dem Leben*, 83 & 151.

quest for formal independence obtained reinforcement from the aims of these same Great Powers. By this time Bleichröder's group as well as all of the Great Powers had only pessimistic evaluations of the likelihood of any further improvement in the status of Romanian Jewry. Article 7 in its revamped guise and the en bloc naturalization of the soldiers seemed all that could be expected short of the use of force majeure. The British and Italians, in particular, reluctantly concealed a growing disquiet behind their pledge of common action with the Germans. Chancellor Bismarck, then, possessed the determinative voice in clearing up the question of Romania's diplomatic status. Once he expressed himself content, the remaining Great Powers would correspondingly endorse his position. In ascending order of importance, therefore, the Romanians had to gauge and appease the hidden agenda as well as the publicly stated aspirations in the matter of Jewish rights of Italy, France, Great Britain, and the German Empire.[46]

For Bismarck's Germany the condition of Romanian Jews and of its own Jewish citizens working there represented only part of the diplomatic equation. Since 1872 considerable pressure had been exerted on the Romanian government by Germany for the awarding of contracts to build that country's railroads. Besides the resentment generated in Bucharest by this harassment, there had existed constant tension on both sides due to the financially precarious nature of the project. This environment had not been helped by the repeated negotiations with the German bankers led by Bleichröder necessary to smooth over the antagonisms and fiscal problems. Bleichröder already possessed considerable standing as an intimate of Bismarck's and a useful adjunct in diplomatic matters. He now surfaced as a principal factor both in the question of extricating German investments from the Romanian rail system and in championing the cause of the Jewish population.[47] By the time of Romania's participation in the Russo-Turkish war of 1877–1878 the difficulties with Germany over the monies invested in the railroads had become critical. In fact during the negotiations

---

[46] Medlicott, "The Recognition of Roumanian Independence," 576–7 & 587; Stern, *Gold and Iron*, 386 & 391.

[47] Stern, *Gold and Iron*, 367 & 369; Medlicott, "The Recognition of Roumanian Independence," 356.

prior to the German-Romanian commercial convention of 1877 a clear link was established between repayment of these sums and the matter of Romanian sovereignty. From this point on the question of expeditious repurchase of the railroads by the Romanian government would become more and more prominent. As in the negotiations and text of the commercial treaty the link between the two German points of attack was only hinted at in the beginning,[48] but by the period immediately after the Congress of Berlin the Romanian government felt itself to be under much more than routine diplomatic pressure. The dynamic between equal rights for its Jewish inhabitants and the railroad issue came into play in a more unmistakable fashion. As one Romanian historian has phrased it, ". . . the inclusion of this article [i.e., Art. XLIV] gave Bismarck a means of blackmailing the Romanian government into buying back the railroads. . . ." By insisting on a literal interpretation of this injunction Berlin could garner enormous leverage in its dealings with Bucharest. Ultimately the Romanians had to pay several times the worth of the railroads, at least in their view, in order to placate Bismarck. This, however, constituted the price of obtaining German acquiescence in the Romanian version of the equal rights for minorities mandated by the Great Powers. And without Bismarck's approval recognition of Romania's independence from any of the other major Western states would not be forthcoming. The interchange between Bucharest and Berlin in this regard, then, illustrated the core of Romania's practical expression of its anti-Semitism. It likewise provided an insight into Romanian intentions for the future and the degree of cynicism brought to the bargain by the Great Powers, Germany in particular.[49]

By January of 1879 the Romanians became increasingly conscious of Bleichröder's importance both as a representative of German investment interests and as the leading spokesman for the Jewish rights issue. In the early spring German diplomats made it quite apparent that the ability of Bleichröder's German investors to recover their funds had become linked

---

[48] *Independenţa României, Documente*, IV, 191; *Nouveau recueil général de Traités et autres actes relatifs aux rapports de droit international*. Continuation du grant recueil de G. Fr de Martens par Jules Hopf. Ser. 2, VIII (Göttingen: Librairie de Dieterich, 1883), 243.
[49] Adǎniloaie, "Berlin," 231–2.

in the widest sense to Romania's welfare. In this instance both sides clearly understood that well being in terms of the resolution of the Jewish question and the granting of formal independence. For some delegates to the constituent assembly the hints delivered had been so inelegant as to stir up fears of new concessions for the Jews being demanded. Shortly after the opening of the constitutional revision assembly in June, Bleichröder expressed himself even more clearly on the price of Romanian independence. Speaking he said for his government's concerns, Bleichröder announced that Berlin now coupled the Jewish question with that of the German railroad investments. For Romania this meant that the conditions for independence imposed by the Congress would not be considered fulfilled until both these matters had been completely cleared up. Indeed the original requirement was to the effect that they had to be settled simultaneously.[50] Making the point personally and unmistakably Bismarck informed the Romanians that Article 44 of the Congress of Berlin formed an integral part of the corpus of international law. A small state could ignore such exigencies only at its peril. None too subtly he reminded them of their precarious strategic position "between two powerful and equally dangerous neighbors" as well as their need for friends. They must, therefore, carry out the prerequisites to independence found in Article 44. In a ploy designed to prod the Romanians on the railroad issue, Bismarck went on to say that the insistence on the equal rights issue came mainly from France and Italy. Germany acquiesced in this suit because of the humanitarian principle involved and the diplomatic awkwardness of not complying with the other two Powers' wishes. He further baited the hook with the observation that he was aware of the great number of Jews involved. The chancellor assumed that such a grave question must be resolved in stages, not precipitously. If Romania would settle to German satisfaction the matter of the one hundred million Marks invested in her railroads, then the relations between the two states would mend immediately. Moreover, the general security of Romania would improve. In brief, once having

[50] "Titu Maiorescu to Jacob C. Negruzzi," Letter of 16 January 1879. *Studii și Documente Literare*, Vol. I, I. E. Toroutiu & Gh. Cardas (eds.), (București: Institutul de Arte Grafice "Bucovina," 1931), 11–3; *Aus dem Leben*, 189 & 215; Gh. Cazan, "Recunoașterea internațională a independenței de Stat a României," *Reprezentanțele Diplomatice ale României*, I (1859–1917), (București: Editura Politică, 1967), 46–7.

addressed the interwoven motifs of Jewish rights and the repurchase of the railroads, Romania would find herself independent and backed up by her "natural friends."[51]

If it had been possible to misunderstand the hints being conveyed by the German representatives, all remaining doubts as to the true substance of the contest over Romanian independence disappeared due to a letter from Prince Carol's father. In early September Karl Anton wrote his son that the railroad issue constituted the overwhelmingly important item for Germany. In his judgment, later borne out in the diplomatic denouement, "The Jewish question . . . [was] more a pretext than a goal." This inference received repeated reinforcement through Berlin's pledges to support Romanian interests once its had been properly consulted. By the late fall of 1879, as hard pressed as the Romanians were and as desperately as they desired formal independence, they also knew that Bismarck felt considerable and mounting pressure. The other Great Powers wanted to bring the prolonged struggle to a conclusion. The German Chancellor had to use his leverage on the Romanians now or perhaps lose the chance to extricate the German investment. The ultimatum sent to Bucharest was rather simple; namely, either the railroad investment was to be recouped immediately or the Jewish rights issue of Article XLIV would be declared unsatisfactorily observed by the Romanians. The first option meant Great Power acceptance as completely independent, while the second precluded such. The Romanians read the message clearly and cleverly. They obviously had to pay the sum coveted by the German bankers, but Prince Carol and his government knew that they had some slight bargaining power now. The Italian government had announced its intention to accredit an ambassador to Bucharest. The Romanians felt confident that Great Britain would follow suit in the near future. Should the common front against recognition collapse, Bismarck would lose his one great hold on the Romanians. For this reason, the Romanian regime concluded that the chancellor would have to tread more softly. They might possibly arrive at an informal understanding on the execution of the Jewish issue.[52]

---

[51] *Aus dem Leben*, 232–5.

[52] Berkowitz, *La Question des Israélites en Roumanie*, 663–5 & 668; *Aus dem Leben*, 247, 266–9 & 271–4.

Italy's attempt to recognize Romanian independence without waiting for Germany to do so constituted a major setback for Bismarck. He had had to deal with the Italians before, in 1878, when they wanted to grant formal recognition as soon as the Bucharest government had revised Article 7 of its constitution. Throughout the wrangling over the railroads, Berlin had been extremely conscious of the need to present a common front, otherwise German investments might be forfeit. Already contemptuous of earlier Italian desires to recognize Romania—branding them a less than respectable policy—Bismarck on this occasion asked France for "a service to which he attached a great price." Recognition by the Italians had given the Romanians the idea that they would not have to accommodate Germany in the matter of the railways investment. Bismarck requested France to notify the Romanian government that along with Great Britain she remained united with Germany on the Jewish issue as defined in Article XLIV.[53] Thus, France, Great Britain, and the reluctant Italians toed the line for Bismarck. The abortive Italian recognition in the first week of 1879 did, however, indicate that Romania had some leeway in dealing with him. As long as the Romanians gave him his main prize, the railroad venture capital, they might dicker on the Jewish issue. They would once more be able to balance between the Powers and in so doing serve their own essential self-interest on the Jewish issue. If they did not prevail where the railroads were concerned, they could conceivably make a sham of Article XLIV. Though not a cost free maneuver, it represented the lesser of the two evils in the Hobson's choice with which the Romanians saw themselves confronted.[54]

By the end of 1879 the combination of bullying by Bismarck and intimations that informal adjustments might be possible wore the Romanians down. They saw absolute economic and social disaster, if Article XLIV were interpreted literally. They also perceived that Bismarck could be brought to trade his prin-

---

[53] Cazan, "Recunoașterea internațională," 32 & 43; *Documents diplomatiques français (1871–1914)*, 1ʳᵉ série (1871–1900), V. 2 (Paris: Imprimerie Nationale, 1930), 402, 467–8, 516, 524, & 597.

[54] Bossy, *Politica externă a României*, 209–10; Bărbulescu, *Reprezentanțele diplomatice*, 49; Martin Winckler, "Bismarcks Rumänienplitik und die Durchführung des Artikels 44 des Berliner Vertrages (1878–1880)," Ph.D. Dissertation (Ludwig-Maximilians-Universität zu München, 1951), 173.

cipled stand on Jewish rights for discharge of the economic issue.[55] In tying the repurchase of the railways to domestic policies, the Germans offered repeated assurances that they had no intention of dictating how Romanian internal affairs were effectuated in practice. As long as the railroad question and the treatment of their own nationals were guaranteed they would be content. All Romania had to do was demonstrate some progress in the area of equal rights for the Jews. Bismarck's spokesmen developed the theme that this combination of actions would prove very profitable on both the political and financial levels. They argued that the recalcitrance of France and Great Britain that was holding up diplomatic recognition of Romania would be overcome by Germany's indication of willingness to accept Bucharest's performance regarding Article XLIV.[56] In the end the matter of equal rights for Romania's Jews became for Bismarck a somewhat devalued humanitarian means to an overriding economic end. The standard shifted merely to declaring an intent to observe the principle established at Berlin. The Romanians would then be left to work out the details as long as they did not seem to be arbitrary. The German government countenanced laws limiting full equality as well as the notion that for the majority of Romanian Jews emancipation would have to be a gradual affair. Berlin found restrictions tolerable as long as the Romanian government exhibited a sufficient degree of sincerity on the theoretical plane and directly offered citizenship to a small number of Jews. German spokesmen made the Romanians fully aware of the threat of Bismarck's displeasure should this imbroglio not be terminated shortly. The leaders in Bucharest also understood that they would have some liberty where interpretation and subsequent constraint of Jewish rights were concerned. In discussing the proposed constitutional change that would require each naturalization to be approved separately by the Romanian legislature, the Romanians acknowledged that requests by Jews for citizenship could be refused. Despite knowing Romania's history on this point and having previously ques-

---

[55] Richard V. Burks, "Romania and the Balkan Crisis of 1875–78," *Journal of Central European Affairs*, 2(1942), nr. 2, 319; Stern, *Gold and Iron*, 371 & 392; Cazan, "Recunoașterea internațională," 47.

[56] *Independența României, Documente*, IV, 491–2, 513, & 582–4.

tioned her intentions, the German government in late 1879 said it found no difficulty with this stance.[57]

Bleichröder had noted almost a year previously that, despite Bismarck's call for a complete emancipation of Romania's Jews, the chancellor would probably settle for less. How much less he did not realize, for besides worrying about the prospect of enormous financial losses by German aristocrats, Bismarck also saw in Article XLIV a means of furthering his foreign policy objectives. At the very least he hoped to consolidate French-German relations. In a more ambitious vein he had in mind a project to be advanced by the purchase he possessed in Article XLIV. He proposed to prove Germany's indispensability to Austria-Hungary and Russia where these states' objectives in Eastern Europe were involved. So by the fall of 1879 the other Great Powers noticed that Bismarck's real interest centered on the railroads and that his antagonism towards Bucharest became overstated. And on all sides the impression grew that his real aims had nothing to do with the outcome of Romanian independence or constitutional minutiae. Bismarck had, of course, earlier expressed disdain for Romania as well as the conviction that her government would attempt to avoid granting true equality of rights to the Jews, but now his fears that the Great Powers might be tricked by the Romanians no longer assumed the same paramount character.[58] By the end of January 1880 the Romanian parliament had passed the bill authorizing the repurchase of the rail system from the German investors represented by Bleichröder. To clear up any lingering doubts about the sense of this legislation, the parliament satisfied the German Foreign Office's request for a clarification. It unequivocally specified that the offer was unconditional and binding. On 6 February the German bankers accepted the railroad convention as completely meeting their requirements. Bismarck, true to his implied bargain with the Romanians, immediately informed the French and British that Berlin now felt itself inclined to accredit an ambassador to Bucharest. The Romanians had achieved their prime goal and felt in a markedly

[57] Iancu, *Les Juifs en Roumanie*, 178; *Independenţa României, Documente*, 502, 524, 563, & 589.

[58] Winckler, "Bismarcks Rumänienpolitik," 106, 112–4, 132–3, & 201; *Documents diplomatiques français (1871–1914)*, V. 2, 401–2, 467, & 524.

improved position. They directed their diplomatic representatives to inform the Western capitals that they would accept nothing less than unconditional recognition. No further provisos or restrictions regarding Romanian independence, certainly not on the matter of Jewish rights, would be allowed. One of the ironies of the situation which the Romanians did not miss was the outbreak of anti-Semitism in Germany at this time. As Karl Anton wrote to Prince Carol, Germany's reputation suffered some obloquy in pressing another state to live up to the standard of Article XLIV while such disturbances occurred on her own domestic scene. But in spite of that supposedly humanitarian pressure the Romanian government had succeeded in its original intent; namely, to preserve what it saw as the national economic and social pattern, while pledging itself only to an abstract policy of guaranteed religious freedom. It had circumvented the use of categories which would have insured the naturalization of far more Jews and managed to substitute individual grants of citizenship.[59]

The British position on the questions of Romanian independence and Jewish rights had its origin in rather different evaluations and concerns. Most of these are most interestingly reflected in the correspondence of Sir William White. White, who became the informal British "minister" in Bucharest in 1878, at first had no title or rank. We can gauge the crucial nature of his legation in the diplomacy of Great Britain in part by the extraordinarily rapid career progress he made once the Court of St. James recognized Romanian independence. White catapulted from the status of consul-general to the second most senior category in the British system, minister-plenipotentiary. Whitehall clearly appreciated the import of his advice regarding the Romanian scene. In rendering this yeoman service, White also provided an incisive judgment on the nature of Romanian bias and the intentions of the government. At the beginning of his tenure in Bucharest, the Foreign Office wrote White explaining that it fully expected Romanian independence to be granted. This suited British designs in the region. The foreign secretary, Lord Salisbury, reminded him at the same time that a prime goal in the Principalities for the British Empire

---

[59] *Aus dem Leben*, 221–2, 283 & 287–90.

was a favorable commercial treaty. Or as the foreign secretary
put it, ". . . We are a nation of shop-keepers and that the only
sure way to our affections is through a liberal tariff."[60] The
British Foreign Office was also very much aware of Russian
desires in the area and not surprised at the retaking of Bessarabia. Though not willing to resist Russia on this territorial
claim, London did want to bolster Romania's position. The
British sought to do so through speedy, formal recognition
as well as other means in order to prevent further Russian
encroachments in the Balkans. With the greatest trust in White's
judgment, Lord Salisbury warily watched not only the Russians, but also the character of his own diplomacy. With strategic
advantage and commercial relations at risk, White and the
British treaded lightly enough so as not to seem too unfriendly
to the Romanians. They did not want the revision of Article
7 of the Romanian constitution or any other issue to occasion
an irreparable breach. While sympathetic to the French attitude on Article XLIV of the Congress of Berlin and the whole
issue of religious toleration, the British, like the Germans, had
more than just those issues on their mind.[61]

As with the other Western Great Powers, Great Britain began
in 1879 insisting that Romania fulfill the requirements laid down
by the Congress of Berlin, in particular, the Romanian constitution had to change to allow for the naturalization of Romania's
Jewish population. Britain, along with France and Germany
for their respective reasons, stood out from the other Great
Powers as being far more adamant on the matter of Jewish rights.
At least for the purposes of the initial diplomatic feints, she
followed a policy of advocacy. Certainly the reports circulated
by White from Bucharest did nothing to alter the suspicious
British perceptions of what the Romanians were about or of
the degree to which British foreign policy objectives might be
served by the common stance on Article XLIV. The British
minister in Bucharest discussed in some persuasive detail how
". . . a Roumanian might become a Jew, yet it was quite impossible for a Jew to become a Roumanian."[62] In January 1879 the
then British ambassador to Paris, Lord Richard Lyons, reported

---

[60] H. Sutherland Edwards, *Sir William White* (London: John Murray, 1902), 134–5.
[61] Ibid., 136; Stern, *Gold and Iron*, 382; Winckler, "Bismarcks Rumänienpolitik," 102.
[62] *Aus dem Leben*, 161; Edwards, *Sir William White*, 160, 166, & 169.

to the foreign secretary that the president of the Romanian Chamber of Deputies (C. A. Rosetti) had visited him with a letter of introduction from White. Rosetti made all the standard Romanian arguments regarding the Jewish situation including the willingness to promulgate religious toleration forthwith. The point that notably impressed Lord Lyons involved Rosetti's adamant stance that virtually all the Jews in Romania were aliens. Despite Lyons's observation that the hold on Romanian independence was caused solely by the delay in meeting the prescriptions of Article 44, Rosetti would commit to no more than "increased facilities" for the future naturalization of Jews. By this time, then, London fully apprehended the Romanian attitude towards the Jewish minority as well as that government's legalistic ploys. In late January Lord Salisbury informed White that any revision of Article 7 permitting only individual applications for naturalization (i.e., a lack of approval by categories which would naturalize considerable numbers at a time) would be unacceptable. If Bucharest wanted recognition, more would have to be done to satisfy the prerequisites of Article XLIV of the Congress of Berlin. London was especially on its guard because White had related a Romanian version of the double standard for Jews. Bucharest treated all Jews as foreigners for purposes of civil and political rights while compelling them to perform the citizen's duty of serving in the army. This duplicity coupled with the fact that many of the families in the Jewish population had lived in Romania for generations obviously portended something less than enthusiastic good will on Bucharest's part.[63]

British awareness of the depth and history of Romanian antipathy to the Jews received reinforcement, when White forwarded to Lord Salisbury extracts from the 1864 law. This information also illustrated the legal mechanisms customarily employed to frustrate Jewish naturalization efforts. When compared to the proposed revision of Article 7 of the Romanian constitution (obtained by the foreign secretary in July 1879), the similarities in tone and substance could not be missed. Besides the extremely bureaucratic nature of the process, the

---

[63] "Correspondence relative to the Independence," *British and Foreign State Papers*, 1137, 1140, & 1145.

suggested alteration obviously did not meet the British mandated minimum of some few naturalizations by categories.
Given White's sage reports, this intransigence on the Romanians' part came as no surprise. In the spring of 1879 he had
informed Lord Salisbury that no Romanian government would
ever acquiesce in the interpretation of Article XLIV which the
Western Great Powers demanded in their inaugural approaches.
Indeed he advanced the opinion that Bucharest would resist
to the end and most bitterly the naturalization of any significant
portion of the Jewish community. His subsequent judgment
on the matter, then, reflected the increasingly practical nature
of London's dealings with the Romanians. Should the Great
Powers continue to postulate such a sweeping capitulation on
Romania's part (i.e., mass naturalization), they would have
to be prepared to wait indefinitely to wrap up the matter of
recognition. At this point, the tenor of White's letter switched
from merely describing the adamantine character of Romanian
prejudice in this affair to estimating the consequences of the
quandary. He specifically warned the foreign secretary regarding the possible loss of the commercial treaty as well as on
the strategic implications of a diplomatic stalemate. He concluded with the prediction that the Romanians would not conform on the issue of equal rights. At the same time White counseled that further delay in accommodating Bucharest on the
independence question might "be found inconvenient."[64]

By March of 1879 British diplomatic efforts became increasingly pragmatic in fashioning overtures to the Romanians. They
divined full well what the Romanians wanted to do regarding
equal rights, and Bucharest would continue to pursue a mas-
querade throughout the spring and summer. Romanian statements on the scope of this alien Jewish "invasion" became even
more elaborate and alarmist. They increasingly underscored
the associated disturbances and the potential damage to the
new state. Furthermore, all the other Great Powers had felt
awkward from the beginning in refusing Romania formal recognition, since the Ottoman Sultan had already accredited a
legation. Great Britain deemed its position even more unten-
able now. Having been *de facto* independent since the signing
of the Treaty of San Stefano, Romania could not be denied

---

[64] Ibid., 1143 & 1147–9.

much longer. Whatever her obstinate reinterpretation of the decisions of Berlin, she manifestly did exist as a separate political entity.[65] In March the British ambassador to Berlin, Lord Odo Russell, bluntly advised the Romanians simply to adopt the principle of equal rights. If they did so in an ostentatious fashion, then ". . . we [the British] will close our eyes to the execution." In more restrained and politic language Lord Lyons repeated this recommendation in July. If the Romanians would proceed to incorporate Article XLIV into their constitution "at the very least in substance," Great Britain would consider this a sufficient commitment to the principles proclaimed at Berlin. Diplomatic relations could be established immediately. By the autumn of 1879 the British were, for the most part, waiting on Bismarck and the railroads issue. A strong current of opinion existed in their Foreign Office that the matter should be expedited. They did have a debt to pay to the German chancellor in an area of relatively little concern to themselves. But the British likewise believed that nothing would truly be affected by the mere removal of a few words from the Romanian constitution. They wanted to terminate the business soon and with as much gain to their own interests as possible. Sir Henry Elliot, British ambassador to Vienna, wrote to White in mid December saying that the Great Powers had ". . . pretty much made up their minds to pretend to be satisfied with what has been done upon that matter [i.e., religious toleration], though of course no one is really satisfied." Elliot agreed with White's earlier assessment that a purely German matter, one having nothing to do with equality of rights, continued to impede the increasingly pressing recognition issue. It now approached the time to mend relations with Bucharest and to act.[66]

During the late summer of 1879 Lord Salisbury continued to find the tactics and proposals of the Romanians unsatisfactory. From the British point of view everything Romania declared herself willing to do in the area of toleration savored of condescension towards a favored few. But beyond "an act of grace towards certain individuals" the British foreign sec-

---

[65] Edwards, *Sir William White*, 162; "Correspondence relative to the Independence," *British and Foreign State Papers*, 1149-56.
[66] *Independenţa României, Documente*, IV, 483 & 557; Edwards, *Sir William White*, 161 & 173-4.

retary did not see in Romanian pronouncements any inclination to embrace the basic concept of equal rights. If anything,
this conclusion was confirmed by the diplomatic circulars broadcast at that time by Bucharest. The Romanian foreign service
persisted in presenting alibi after alibi to justify existing conditions and to preclude any essential change. On the one hand
Bucharest's diplomats contended that Romania did in fact
espouse the humanitarian thrust of Article XLIV. Then they
engaged in semantic games about the nature of naturalization;
namely, that it could only be an individual act, not a collective
one accomplished through categories. Finally they maintained
that the practical execution of equal rights could only be "within
the limits of the possible." Romanian apprehensions on the
socioeconomic plane and their claims relative to the backwardness of the Hasidic émigrés continued unabated. The unambiguous attitude here left no doubt in the British mind as to
how circumscribed those possibilities were likely to be. The
Romanians would study the question and legalize a few individual naturalizations. Beyond this they held fast to their con-
ventional position that they could accomplish no more than
passage of a law giving citizenship to a nominal list of patently
assimilated Jews.[67] Lord Salisbury, writing to White in Bucharest at this time, labeled all that the Romanians guaranteed
under Article XLIV "an illusory concession." While being very
cognizant of the emptiness of Romanian promises in this area,
however, Salisbury also accepted their argument on the difficulties of Jewish emancipation. Playing to the Romanian initiative he endorsed a gradual implementation of religious toleration. He specifically told White that "immediate application
so far as was feasible" of the principles of Article XLIV would
meet British requirements. To the Romanian ear "feasible"
resounded very much like their own shibboleth, "within the
limits of the possible." Then in September 1879 White relayed
to London his final judgment that nothing more would be forthcoming from the Romanians on the Jewish issue. Beyond the
grudging concessions of the revised Article 7 with its provision for individual naturalization, they would only sanction
a one time en bloc granting of citizenship to *selecti quidem*. If

---

    [67] "Correspondence relative to the Independence," *British and Foreign State Papers*,
1157–62.

Great Britain and the other Great Powers demanded more than this, they would have to coerce Romania through the use of force. White asserted that the depth of anti-Semitism and nationalistic sentiment in the country assured the rejection of any proposal exceeding the boundaries of this compromise.[68]

By the late fall London eagerly watched the German-Romanian discussions on the repurchase of the railway system. The British, though resigned to waiting on the approval of Berlin, were more anxious than ever to regularize relations with Romania. All further delay seemed unwise. In the first week of February 1880, when the pact between Berlin and Bucharest on the railroads reached fruition, the British acted immediately. They informed the French that they believed no further purpose would be served in delaying formal recognition of Romanian independence any longer. Foreign Secretary Salisbury's note even included a suggestion that the Great Powers imply to Bucharest that they have ". . . full confidence that by a liberal execution of it [i.e., revised Article 7] they will bring the operation of their law into exact conformity with the spirit of the Treaty of Berlin." Though a pious hope, it had been well refuted by the Romanians and judged otherwise by the British in advance of recognition. Indeed, by the early spring of 1880, the British were both tired of the situation and desirous of cultivating amicable relations with the Romanians. Though fully aware of the results of the constitutional bargain, London informed White that the Romanians should not be offended any further on this score. The British relapsed into a sanguine trust that gradually more would be done for the Jews. With Bismarck at ease on the investment question and other foreign policy considerations looming more pressingly on the British agenda, the question of Jewish equality in Romania was defined as passably settled.[69]

While the Germans maneuvered for the railroads and the British sought their commercial arrangement, both ultimately found it difficult to facilitate simultaneously their own interests and the status of the Romanian Jews. The French, however, pursued a less convoluted policy. Though by the fall of

---

[68] Ibid., 1165–6, 1168, 1176.
[69] Ibid., 1179–80; *Documents diplomatiques français (1871–1914)*. 1re série (1871–1900), V. 3. (Paris: Imprimerie Nationale, 1931), 15; Edwards, *Sir William White*, 174.

1879 they too thought the moment opportune to recognize Romania's independence, France had been firmly committed from the beginning to common action with Germany and Great Britain. The French government would proceed with formal acknowledgment of Romanian sovereignty only when the others assented to move on the question. The Paris regime had also from the inception of this contest had to be concerned with its image and the matter of consistency in its foreign policy. Given both her political traditions and her stance on the humanitarian issue of equality of rights during the Congress of Berlin, France could not now seem to be abandoning concepts or practices defended so vigorously in the past.[70] Her dilemma, like that of the other two Western Great Powers, consisted in the fact that she had known all along that the Romanians would probably try to avoid their obligations under Article XLIV. France wanted to recognize Romanian sovereignty as well as present an untarnished front on the question of toleration. Early in 1879, then, the French government decided that it could "content itself with a formal commitment" from Bucharest on the issue of religious rights. Paris required merely a pledge backed up by some material action to prove the sincerity of the Romanians. Foreign Minister Waddington held until the end of the discussions on Romanian independence that Article XLIV should ideally result in categories of Jews being established. Individuals encompassed by these groupings would there and then become citizens. By late summer 1879, however, he would settle for much less. For the explicit gesture on equality of rights he would now accept an "equivalent statement."[71]

As an evincement of Romanian goodwill, Waddington hoped to see approximately two thousand of the Jewish community admitted to citizenship immediately. The French egregiously underestimated the depth and force of Romanian religious rancor, though Bucharest's words and actions did more than enough to make these unmistakable. As we have already seen, Bucharest provided the long awaited proof of its genuineness

---

[70] "Correspondence relative to the Independence," *British and Foreign State Papers*, 180; *Independenţa României, Documente*, IV, 427.

[71] *Documents diplomatiques français*, V. 2, 402 & 466-8; Correspondence relative to the Independence," *British and Foreign State Papers*, 1157.

by granting citizenship to barely half the number Waddington expected. At the time of their formal recognition of Romanian independence, the French received a final display of this recalcitrance. For by this time Bucharest's unwillingness to put anything on paper that might serve as a liberal precedent in Jewish matters had escalated markedly. Like the Germans and the Italians, the French exhibited some anxiety over the status of their nationals of Jewish origin resident in the new Kingdom of Romania. They sought an official clarification, therefore, that all French citizens would continue to have the legal opportunity to acquire rural real estate. Even though this might have been the occasion for some display of artfulness towards a friendly Great Power and of some magnanimity in a successfully settled affair of prime importance, the Romanians held fast to a strengthened and more highly articulated anti-Semitism. Refusing to pledge anything more on the level of principle, the Romanian government would go no farther than to state that in practice no one would have any problems in this regard, "except for the Jews." France had waited too long to obtain this type of explicit concession. With Romania now independent she could achieve neither the results of the German and Italian commercial conventions nor the most favored nation guarantee for citizens' rights which the British attained in their commercial treaty of 1880.[72]

While Germany, Great Britain, and France cast the determinative ballots on Romanian independence, Italy too had a role to play. The Italians were not only extremely conscious of the ethnic connection and of the similarities between their and the Romanians' recent national developments, but also felt very much predisposed to aid them whenever possible. They went out of their way to cultivate their Danubian cousins, telling them that they constituted one of the major civilizing influences in the Balkans. This catering to Romanian nationalism was reciprocated in Bucharest's frequent bows in the direction of racial affinities and appreciation for Italy's unusual initiative in bolstering Romanian diplomatic efforts. The original Italian position on Romanian independence (i.e., that there

---

[72] *Documents diplomatiques français* V. 3, 10; Ion Ionașcu, Petre Bărbulescu, and Gheorghe Gheorghe (eds.), *Tratatele internaționale ale României, 1354–1920* (București: Editura Științifică și Enciclopedică, 1975), 235–6.

should be no preconditions to recognition), of course, reinforced the line taken by the Danubian government. More importantly for the anti-Semitic issue it helped strengthen Bucharest's determination throughout this period.[73] In practical terms, though, Rome continued to be most cautious. This initial urge to grant recognition was held in check by the designs of the other Great Powers. Despite the urgency of the Romanian diplomatic exertions in Rome, the Italian government proceeded with what it termed the prudent course of action. Rome meant to limit itself at the most to the signing of a commercial convention, but it also attempted to persuade the other Great Powers that, while perhaps Bucharest should make some allowances in the realm of Jewish rights, they were primarily hurting themselves. Romania had obtained de facto independence the moment her former sovereign, the Ottoman Empire, signed the Treaty of San Stefano. All that was now being accomplished by insisting on Article XLIV was the squandering of valuable influence. The Italians used what lobbying capacity they possessed to try to influence the Germans' course of action, in this instance through the offices of the British. They would, for the moment, remain in the fold, but were not pleased with doing so.[74]

Rome became for the Romanians, well before the 1877 war and the subsequent struggle over independence, the principal focus of their diplomatic maneuvers. With the establishment of a diplomatic agency in Rome in April of 1873, the Italians accorded the Bucharest government a limited level of official support if not acceptance among the concert of European powers. They also allowed the Romanians an arena for the dissemination of propaganda calculated to stimulate interest in, if not official support of, their nationalistic goals.[75] But even such circumspect diplomatic underpinning did assist the Romanians over the course of the tumultuous 1879–1880 period. At the same time it provided them with valuable intelligence into how to handle the toleration issue. In the commercial convention they not only granted Romania a closer relationship, but in protecting their own Jewish citizens went some distance in

---

[73] Bărbulescu, *Reprezentanțele diplomatice*, 32; Bossy, *Politica externă a României*, 162, 189, 210.

[74] *Aus dem Leben*, 129–33; Bossy, *Politica externă*, 59, 78, 154–6; "Correspondence relative to the Independence," *British and Foreign State Papers*, 1146.

[75] Bărbulescu, *Reprezentanțele diplomatice*, 241, 244 & 247–8; Bossy, *Politica externă*, 1–3.

trying to impress upon Bucharest the concerns of Western Europe. This "politics of prudence" on the Italian part included a prolonged effort to tutor the Romanians on the deleterious effect on foreign public opinion their anti-Semitic legislation produced.[76] As early as 1875 and 1876 Roman spokesmen made a point of linking any possibility of Romania's achieving the status of an independent European state with some modification in this area. There even ensued an unsuccessful endeavor on the Italians' part to convince the Romanians that the eventual assimilation of their Jews could be in their own best interest. Ultimately the Italian spokesmen conveyed to the Romanians that their deportment would have to take into consideration the realities of Roman political life. Specifically they highlighted the fact that influential members of both the Italian parliament and press were of Jewish ancestry. Then they insisted that an obdurate Romanian stance made it difficult for the most willing of their Roman advocates to risk the political consequences of actively backing them. Unfortunately, over the course of the negotiations for Romanian independence these admonitions would have an effect diametrically opposed to that intended. Repeated Italian remonstrances regarding the "power of the Jews on all the European cabinets" and that "the Jews are extremely powerful among us [i.e., the Italians]" simply confirmed in the Romanian mind the existence of a Jewish conspiracy to frustrate their drive for independence. Whether meant or not this type of advice from the Italian foreign ministry played both to the Romanian sense of aggrievement against the Jews and to the all too familiar stereotype of a baleful Jewish influence on public affairs.[77]

The Romanians quite naturally watched for any and all signs in Italian political life that their position would be accepted wholesale and result in recognition. Occasionally the voice of a splinter faction did emerge endorsing the stand that consitutional issues represented a purely domestic matter. Unfortunately for the more diehard Romanian anti-Semites, the Italian government consistently advised Bucharest to render at least

---

[76] *Nouveau recueil général de Traités*, VIII, 608–9; Bărbulescu, *Reprezentanţele diplomatice*, 245–7.

[77] Bossy, *Politica externă*, 28–31, 125, & 134–40; Cecil Roth, *The History of the Jews of Italy* (Philadelphia: The Jewish Publication Society of America, 1946), 476.

token acknowledgment of the humanitarian substance of Article XLIV. Rome urged the Romanians to seem to make a commitment on the requirements of the Congress of Berlin or to fabricate the semblance of such a pronouncement. The Italians clearly told the Romanian government that they were looking for a "moral engagement" not a legal one where Jewish rights were concerned. Without such, Romania would continue to suffer in Italian public opinion especially when compared to Serbia. It would also be impossible for any of the Great Powers to proceed with recognition or even to initiate any new measures to assist Romania.[78] The Italian diplomats engaged in these negotiations stressed that their Jewish community harbored deep suspicions that the Romanians intended to take back with one hand what they gave to the Jews with the other. In particular, if Romania's Jews were not naturalized en bloc, then the simple enshrinement of tolerant language in the constitution signified little. Bucharest had to provide in the manner of its revision of Article 7 some pretext for Italy and the other Great Powers to act. All of these states required a cover allowing the various governments to assuage their own sensibilities and the passions of their citizens. Although Italy wished to lead the way in recognizing Romania's independence, it could not risk being the first to do so unless Bucharest cooperated through the development of a suitable stratagem.[79]

In the end, Italian counsel would prevail; namely, to give formal adherence to Article XLIV's demand for equality of rights, while reserving the full implementation of these until later. Rome repeatedly advocated what came to be the Romanian plan. After embracing the principle of tolerance, execution would be left to regulation by legislative action. The Romanians interpreted this advice as consonant with their nationalistic goals. They also perceived it as a sanction of their determination to stand their ground against any sweeping and meaningful enactment of an equal rights provision. The Romanians read this admonition in the light of their own self-interest and predilections. Thus they maintained that, having inscribed religious toleration with its political overtones in the constitution, they had given practical expression to the spe-

---

[78] Bossy, *Politica externă*, 183, 188–90.
[79] *Independenţa României, Documente*, IV, 536–7; Bossy, *Politica externă*, 194–8.

cifications of Berlin. Other than the mass granting of naturalization to approximately one thousand assimilated Romanian Jews, they had to do nothing additional.[80]

One of the ironically interesting scenarios of the Italian-Romanian diplomatic jockeying during 1878–1879 involved the role played by Giacomo Malvano (chief of the political division of the Italian Ministry of Foreign Affairs). For several decades Malvano, a Piedmontese of Jewish origins, served as a major participant in Italian international negotiations of all types. The Romanian diplomatic agents in Rome quickly picked up on and reported to Bucharest that they had to work through an Italian Jew in their efforts to obtain Rome's recognition.[81] Malvano, according to the Romanian estimation, was a man of considerable competence and influence. Most importantly he represented the conduit through which the Italian foreign minister channeled Bucharest's diplomatic agents when dealing with Rome on the linked issues of recognition and Jewish rights. Malvano brought home to the Romanian agent with no possibility for misunderstanding his government's poor impression of the debates on revising Article 7. He likewise expressed his own hostility to the tack taken by the Romanian constituent assembly. In early December 1879 the Romanians addressed these antipathies through a note delivered to the Italian minister of foreign affairs. So eager were they by this point to obtain Rome's support that they submitted the draft of this memorandum to the Italians for editing. They hoped in this manner to tailor it better to meet the criticisms of the Italian parliamentary opposition. Despite all that we have seen of their mentality and motivations to this stage, they now pledged not only an endorsement of Article XLIV but also one that would be "sincere and straightforward." The Romanian agent likewise committed his government to an increasingly complete process of assimilation as well as to the eradication of all restrictive measures directed against the Jewish community. In sum, the Romanians produced a sop to Italian governmental concerns which was designed to undercut any further opposition to diplomatic recognition. They assured Malvano and the other

---

[80] Bossy, *Politica externă*, 198–200; Bărbulescu, *Reprezentanţele*, 48.
[81] Roth, *The History of the Jews of Italy*, 478; Bossy, *Politica externă*, 180; Iorga, *Correspondance diplomatique*, 280.

Italian diplomats that the Jews' legal status in Romania would
be guaranteed to the extent of precluding arbitrary bureaucratic
actions against them in the future.[82]

With this gambit played, the Romanian agent could report
on 5 December 1879 that "The question of the recognition of
our independence by Rome can be considered resolved." He
went on to say that this ruse fitted conveniently into the Italian
desire to display the decisiveness and freedom of action of
a Great Power. By taking the initiative to be the first to recognize Romania, Italy could reinforce her own diplomatic situation as well. This action on the part of Rome would also help
make up for earlier Romanian disappointment, when Italian
recognition was not immediately forthcoming.[83] The artifice
worked. Malvano exhibited a more friendly demeanor towards
the Romanian agent after this, while the Italian parliament's
anxieties subsided. Malvano did ask again for assurances in
the area of civil and legal rights regarding situations where
capricious measures by the government might result in abuse
of the Jewish community. The Romanian response once more
resolved itself into one of disingenuousness and a recapitula-
tion of the early promise to assimilate the Jews over time. As
political director of the Ministry of Foreign Affairs, Malvano
in these interviews seemed more concerned with the status
of Italian Jews resident in Romania and trade than in the larger
question of equality of rights guaranteed by the constitution.
On these points both he and his government accepted additional Romanian assurances that fundamentally did no more
than repeat in another form what had already been conceded
by Bucharest. The reiteration, however, had the appearance
of offering something extra and evinced the sincerity Rome
demanded. The Italian Foreign Ministry could now justify its
inclination towards speedy recognition of Romania's independence. The Romanian diplomatic agent in Rome reported to
his foreign minister that this interchange had achieved a signal
impact on relations between Bucharest and Rome. He recounted
his success in convincing the Italians to proceed with recognition on the basis of a declaration of intent to do something
equivocal in the indefinite future. This sums up a great por-

---

[82] Bossy, *Politica externă*, 204.
[83] Ibid.; Rosetti, *C. A. Rosetti*, 312–3.

tion of Romania's diplomacy throughout the struggle over Jewish rights.[84]

As we have already discussed, this precipitous action on the part of Italy greatly irritated Bismarck as well as placed the remaining Great Powers in an impossible position. Italian action did halt temporarily pending the closing of the railroad negotiations between the Germans and Romanians. But the decision to recognize Romanian independence on 6 December 1879 gave the Romanians the confidence needed to deal with Bismarck and to remain resolute in their anti-Semitic interpretation of Article XLIV. Whatever happened they relentlessly applied the humanitarian verbiage according to their own vested interests. Malvano himself consoled the Romanians, when it became necessary to await the conclusion of Bismarck's and Bleichröder's extraction of German investments from Romania. Despite the temporary delay, then, the Romanian government felt it had carried the day and expressed uncommon gratitude for the Italian enterprise. It went out of its way to thank, among others, Director Malvano for his good offices as head of the Political Affairs section of the Italian Foreign Ministry.[85]

By the winter of 1880 all the Great Powers were anxious to dispose of the Romanian issue. The Germans had received all they wanted plus reassurances on the railway investments, and Romania at least as far as surface manifestations counted had undertaken to observe the niceties of religious tolerance and equality of rights. The Great Powers had employed Article XLIV of the Congress of Berlin as a diplomatic means to their own special purposes. Now they declared themselves willing to accept Romania's actions in revising its constitution as full settlement for admission to the European concert of nations.[86] None believed that the reforms went far enough, but demurred at placing any further reservations or stipulations on their recognition of Romania as a completely sovereign state. All that France, Germany, and Great Britain could manage at this terminal stage of the process was to deplore the fact that Bucharest's constitutional revision did not entirely correspond

---

[84] Bossy, *Politica externă*, 206–9.

[85] Ibid., 210–12; "Correspondence relative to the Recognition," *British and Foreign State Papers*, 1179–80.

[86] Medlicott, "The Recognition of Roumanian Independence," 589; Winckler, "Bismarcks Rumänienpolitik," 175.

to their views of what was required by Article XLIV of the Congress of Berlin. In their identical notes of recognition all three Great Powers deplored the necessity of naturalization by individuals rather than through the use of categories for en masse granting of citizenship. This remained in their estimations a glaring deficiency. But, then, the Romanians had designed the procedure to allow themselves exactly this loophole. The British still felt uneasy about the pettiness demonstrated when the Romanians parceled out the approximately one thousand grants of naturalization required to prove their good intentions. Almost any technicality sufficed to have a name removed from the list as not having properly served in the army, acquired the requisite degree, etc., etc.[87] But, finally, on 20 February, 1880 France, Germany, and Great Britain did grant full and formal recognition to what would shortly become the Kingdom of Romania. With these letters of credence delivered to Prince Carol's government, the Italian papers could likewise be accorded completing the diplomatic rites and satisfying Romania's nationalistic aspirations on the level of international relations.[88]

Bucharest won. True, Romania had in the course of attaining independent status been buffeted and even humiliated. And Russia had reclaimed Bessarabia from its erstwhile ally. But in those areas where the country had had some room to maneuver, especially regarding the impact of minority rights on the established sociopolitical order, it conceded nothing of substance. As would be proven in the next four decades by the paltry number of Romanian Jews naturalized, the constitutional revision of Article 7 remained largely decorative. More importantly the existence of an independent Romania and the character of Romanian nationalism now intertwined inseparably with anti-Semitism. The anti-Jewish and politically active intelligentsia produced a logic and rhetoric of this prejudice that equated being Romanian with harboring anti-Semitic ideas. In the debates over the revision of Article 7 and in their writings up to World War I these intellectuals constructed a

---

[87] Seton-Watson, *A History of the Roumanians*, 353; *Aus dem Leben*, 290–4; "Correspondence relative to the Recognition," *British and Foreign State Papers*, 1167 & 1178.

[88] "Correspondence relative to the Recognition," *British and Foreign State Papers*, 1186–88; *Aus dem Leben*, 293–4.

conceptual framework which more rigorously and thoroughly excluded the Jews from membership in the nation than ever before. From independence onwards to be a Romanian nationalist signified that the individual necessarily also was an anti-Semite. We must now turn to hear what this group of cultural and political champions had to say.

The Voice of
the Intelligentsia

In the course of the struggle to obtain independence as well as in the general intellectual life of the nation afterward, anti-Semitism constituted a given, but it also underwent a process of elaboration. For the intelligentsia this prejudice against the Jewish community became more highly defined and identified with the essence of Romanian culture and tradition. Anti-Jewish bias developed beyond the customary, sweeping postulate that there existed a natural diversity of races distinguished by specific differences in character, nature, sentiment, and goals.[1] This xenophobic premise summed up the Romanian intellectual's approach to all the ethnic groups in his region, not just to the Jewish element. In the instance of the Jewish community, however, the conceptual creativity of the intelligentsia, motivated by the emotional force of an extreme form of romantic nationalism, reached the level of chauvinism. They now focused on the Jews with a hostile selectivity not shown to any other ethnic minority in the new nation. Indeed, immediately after the Congress of Berlin, the more outspoken Romanian anti-Semites could not bring themselves to make even a pretense of observing Jewish civil and political rights. The pattern, as already intimated none too subtly in the discussions at Berlin and in the constituent assembly's debates, became one of rationalized evasion. Obstruction became the *modus operandi* wherever minority rights might impinge on

---

[1] Raoul V. Bossy, *Politica externă a României între anii 1873–1880 privită dela Agenția diplomatica din Roma* (București: Cultura Națională, 1928), 124–5.

99

national values. The distrust of the Jewish community for economic and cultural reasons grew, being expressed ever more articulately and by the most august elements in the Romanian pantheon. From mid-century onwards Bleichröder's prediction on the general antipathy of Romanians towards Jews had been borne out with a vengeance in the theories and rant of the anti-Semitic intelligentsia.[2]

In surveying the nineteenth century intelligentsia's development of an ideology of anti-Semitism, we will be struck by how illiberal even the most magnanimous (by Romanian standards, that is) supporters of Jewish rights sound to modern ears. For example, Petre P. Carp (1837–1918) stood out dramatically in the constitutional revision debates. He had the temerity to speak against popular violence and the partisan use of anti-Semitic themes in the party maneuverings of the assembly. But even this most altruistic of Romanian spokesmen for humanitarian values called for only a piecemeal according of rights to the Jewish community.[3] Yet, as we will be seeing, far more extreme statements of what would today be considered pronounced anti-Semitism earned their authors the politically crippling label of "friend of the Jews." We are looking, then, in the period from Romania's war of independence in 1877–1878 until the outbreak of World War I at an intellectual landscape permeated by anti-Jewish feeling. For the modern observer a key element to keep in mind is the central nature of this sentiment in Romanian thought. Equally important will be the degree to which this bias is presented as not only fact, but completely justified in being a part of every educated Romanian's intellectual impedimenta.[4]

In this chapter, then, we will analyze the anti-Semitic thought of six men who exercised determinative sway in establishing the tone for the development of this ideology through the First World War. While others wrote and spoke on the topic as well,

---

[2] R. W. Seton-Watson, *A History of the Roumanians* (Hamden: Archon Books, 1963), 352; Fritz Stern, *Gold and Iron. Bismarck, Bleichröder, and the Building of the German Empire* (New York: Vintage Books, 1979), 372 & 374.

[3] C. Gane, *P. P. Carp, și locul sau in istoria politică a țării*, I (Bucarești: Editura Ziarului "Universal," 1936), 231–2; Carol Iancu, *Les Juifs en Roumanie (1866–1919), de l'Exclusion à l'Emancipation* (Aix-en-Provence: Editions de l'Université de Provence, 1978), 168.

[4] D. Murărasu, *Naționalismul lui Eminescu* (București: Institutul de Arte Grafice "Bucovina" I. E. Toroțiu, 1932), 143–5.

these six belonged then as they do now to the core of Romanian intellectual life. We are not dealing, therefore, with the scabrous fringe but with men whose works still constitute required reading for all members of the nationalistic intelligentsia in Romania. These individuals, five historians and one poet, represented for their contemporaries as well as for subsequent generations the best the country had to offer. Three of these men also served as politicians of signal accomplishments, rising to the nation's highest posts and in the process exerting enormous influence on its evolution. Their works appear regularly in new editions, their names are commemorated in the titles of research institutes and libraries of national importance. Any one receiving an education in Romania since the mid-nineteenth century would have read their writings. Their anti-Semitic influence on the intelligentsia has been monumental. They voiced this prejudice with a memorable panache and in doing so appealed to a basic trait of Romanian nationalism. If men of such stature and talent thought this way, if they equated anti-Semitism with being Romanian and with the fundamentals of the nation's heritage, we cannot be surprised at the continuing impact they have had.

Mihail Kogălniceanu (1817–1891) we have already met in his various guises of foreign minister and politician. Broadening our view to take in his historical and polemical writings we now encounter one of the foremost analysts of Romanian history as well as one of the mildest in a long line of exceptionally vehement Moldavian anti-Semites. Born in the capital of Iași, Kogălniceanu knew first hand the underdeveloped nature of that northern province with its primitive economy and associated social problems. Though most definitely an anti-Semite, his version of this malady did not reflect the full virulence usually associated with its proponents from this region, as we will see in discussing the ideas of Mihai Eminescu and Bogdan Petriceicu Hasdeu. While sharing in the basic values of such militant anti-Jewish spokesmen, Kogălniceanu sketched a slightly less acerbic profile of this motif.[5] His earliest pronouncements on the issue of minority rights do not deal with

---

[5] Ion Bodunescu, *Diplomația românească în slujba independenței* (Iași: Editura Junimea, 1978), 107–110; Teodor Armon, " 'Enemies' and 'Traitors'–Aspects of the Anti-semitism of the Iron Guard," *Romanian Jewish Studies*, 1 (1987), nr. 1: 68.

the Jewish question at all or only in passing. Rather he was concerned with the awarding of legal equality to Christians belonging to sects other than the Eastern Orthodox Church. When speaking in the context of Protestants and Roman Catholics resident in the Danubian Principalities, Kogălniceanu proclaimed that every member of the community was a Romanian. In pursuing the Romanian goals of unification and nationhood, he emphasized that the exclusion of some members of the community could only impede progress in these directions. In particular he stressed that differentiation in the granting of political rights to various groups of inhabitants could only lead to disparate vested interests, communal discord, and hatred. Writing in the period before the Russo-Turkish War of 1877–1878, then, Kogălniceanu advocated a policy of tolerance and equal rights, but only for other types of Christians. Throughout his career he would on occasion make a genuinely humanitarian argument for minority rights. But here he pointed out that the Catholic and Protestant Great Powers would not look benevolently on Romanian aspirations for independence, when their coreligionists suffered under religious disabilities.[6]

Even in this thesis on religious toleration for other varieties of Christians, Kogălniceanu advanced xenophobic arguments stressing the necessity of national homogeneity. These contentions he would later launch against the Jewish community. He categorically rejected the right of any group in the Principalities wishing to be considered Romanian citizens to refer to themselves as a distinct nation. If such groups did not share Romanian hardships and especially if they appealed to an outside power for protection, then they could not be viewed as worthy to enjoy the same rights as Romanians. To be granted equality of rights these ethnic groups must share in the dream of independence and labor for Romania's future just as the native Romanian did. For the Romanian nationalists in the period after the unification of the Principalities in 1859 xenophobia became an integral part of their creed. Whereas the Jew until this time had some chance of being perceived as a

---

6 Mihail Kogălniceanu, "Despre drepturile politice ale străinilor, ale pământenilor de orice religie creștina," *Cuvânt introductiv la cursul de istorie națională și câteva din discursurile in Divanul Ad-Hoc al Moldovei* (București: Librăriei Leon Alcalay, 1909), 66, 71, & 85.

fellow worker in the cause of national unity, afterwards he was transmuted into a symbol for all the socioeconomic tensions racking the two provinces. He became the foreigner who monopolized three-quarters of the avenues of economic opportunity in the land. From 1859 through the end of World War I, the Jews in Romania came to personify for Kogălniceanu as well as other members of the political-cultural intelligentsia a marked danger to their national identity. All of this elite saw their country at risk due to the number of unassimilated Jewish immigrants from the north. The Jew was now hated not only as an alien, but also because he was proclaimed to be a "scourge" preventing the full development of the nation.[7] Even at this early stage, long before the heated debates in the constituent assembly, we can perceive in the supposedly moderate rhetoric of Kogălniceanu the increasingly casual presence of anti-Semitism. Speaking of the number of Jewish immigrants and their alleged domination of the Moldavian economy he referred to them not simply as foreign, but also used the Romanian equivalent of the pejorative "Yid." As we will see, he later employed other variants of this term, all of which carry markedly derogatory connotations not found in the polite form of Romanian.[8] In addition to its traditional implications of "traitor" and "Christ killer," terms such as *Jidani* instead of *Evrei*, when alluding to the Jewish community, carried nationalistic overtones of unacceptability and suspicion. It was indicative of the climate of opinion among the intellectual elite that one of the most balanced voices on minority issues resorted to this argot. Yet in the eyes of the rabid anti-Semites Kogălniceanu, even when comporting himself in this fashion regarding the Jews, still displayed too great a delicacy. Eventually, he suffered the politically awkward if not disastrous accusation of being guilty of "filosemitism." By mid-nineteenth century being fittingly anti-Semitic had become identified with acceptability as a Romanian nationalist.[9]

---

[7] Ibid., 68 & 79; Carol Iancu, *Les Juifs en Roumanie (1866–1919), de l'Exclusion à l'Emancipation* (Aix-en-Provence, 1978), 130–4.

[8] Kogălniceanu, "Despre drepturile politice ale străinilor," 79; Ghitta Sternberg, *Stefanesti, Portrait of a Romanian Shtetl* (Oxford: Pergamon Press, 1984), 221; for a brief survey of Jewish immigration into Romanian territories see, L. S. Stavrianos, *The Balkans Since 1453* (New York: Holt, Rinehart & Winston, 1965), 484.

[9] Bogdan Petriceicu Hasdeu, *Scrieri Literare, Morale și Politice*, II, Mircea Eliade (ed.). (București: Fundația pentru Literatură și Artă "Regele Carol II," 1937), 332.

As in so much of Romanian anti-Semitism so too in the thought of Kogălniceanu there emerged an element of inconsistency both regarding tolerance and his estimation of the Jewish community. When speaking in the abstract on the virtues of tolerating differences of faith, he sounded quite temperate. Like so many of his contemporaries he also viewed Romanian history as having demonstrated an unusual absence of bigotry. Referring once again to the Jews with a pejorative term he maintained that they had always enjoyed full religious liberty. He like others made the precious distinction that the Romanian Principalities had never been the scene of the type of bloody religious wars that had swept across much of Western Europe. Certainly the Jews had not been treated as they had in some other Christian lands. By definition, therefore, there existed a tradition of religious toleration encompassing, among others, the Jews.[10] While true as far as it goes, this distinction did not impress the Jewish advocates of the late 1870s, as we have seen. Furthermore, though decrying discrimination in theory, Kogălniceanu pleaded a nationalism which would later, even in his own works, echo more narrowly when Jewish rights came into dispute, for the prime stress he consistently gave to patriotism, not to the more idealistic values of human equality. Be tolerant so that Europe will aid in Romanian unification and independence! Grant equal rights to further the development of the Romanian nation! There existed a strong utilitarian character to his thought, one characteristic of Romanian anti-Semitism at large. The undercurrent carried with it the palpable nuance that, if Europe was not required for Romanian national goals or if patriotism demanded another view of toleration, then the issue might be expressed in a different manner. The accent always remained on "the interest of the nation." The ameliorating grace consisted in the fact that minority groups such as the Jews might contribute on occasion to the vital affairs of the Romanian people.[11]

Kogălniceanu demonstrated the full range and complexity of his variety of Romanian anti-Semitism in the course of the

---

[10] Mihail Kogălniceanu, "Pentru toleranţa religioasă," *Cuvânt introductiv la cursul de istorie naţională şi câteva din discursurile in Divanul Ad-Hoc al Moldovei* (Bucureşti: Editura Librăriei Leon Alcalay, 1909), 49 & 53–5.

[11] Ibid., 51, 53, & 55–8.

struggle for diplomatic recognition in the years 1877 to 1880. In his exposition of the diplomatic game being played and its interaction with the domestic scene he also amplified a number of themes which would help carry the revision forward. These became characteristic of Romanian bias towards the Jews. As a somewhat moderate anti-Semite and a pragmatist he sustained the position that Romania should accept the consequences of Article XLIV. He championed revising the constitution so that it read in conformity with Western notions of equal rights. He did, of course, consider the whole matter an infringement on his nation's dignity and autonomy. However, Kogălniceanu advised the delegates to the constituent assembly to proceed with the revision so as to prove their sincerity in the matter. Once this was accomplished, they could then regulate the Jewish question in accordance with their views of the national interest. But to have the absolute sovereignty desired they had to pay the price of appearing to meet Europe's demands at least half way. Then they could expend the same energy and wit in addressing the application of these legal changes.[12] Public relations ultimately played a fundamental role in Kogălniceanu's approach to the issue of minority rights. Bucharest had to put the best face possible on a difficult problem, while still continuing to pursue basically the same course. He exhorted the assembly to revise the constitution, but he likewise reminded them that only enough would be done to satisfy simultaneously the inconvenient impositions of the Great Powers and the essential requirements of the nation. Kogălniceanu specifically stated that the editing of the constitution must reflect the defensive concerns of Moldavia with its immense new Jewish population. In this vein he backed the compromise to naturalize a token number of Jews, mostly veterans, and to hedge future naturalizations about with a cumbersome set of Kafkaesque bureaucratic preconditions. Only the most resourceful, persistent, and fortunate Jews would be able to employ this scheme for becoming a Romanian citizen with any hope of success.[13]

---

[12] Mihail Kogălniceanu, *Opere*, IV, Georgeta Penelea (ed.), (Bucureşti: Editura Academiei Republicii Socialiste România, 1978), 488–90, 637, & 640.

[13] Mihail Kogălniceanu, *Opere*, V, Georgeta Penelea (ed.), (Bucureşti: Editura Academiei Republicii Socialiste România, 1984), 147, 150, & 182.

In understanding Kogălniceanu's brand of anti-Semitism and the lasting impact it had on the Romanian intelligentsia we must keep in mind his view of the origins of the Jewish question, especially in his native province of Moldavia. He harped on the fact that the Romanian Principalities had been too generous in allowing easy access to native status. They had all too frequently offered an unconditional hospitality to immigrants fleeing the persecution and turmoil of other areas. Interestingly, he contended that the Jewish question in Romania involved not a matter of principle, but of numbers. If only there were not so many of them, there would be no issue of Jewish rights in Romania according to Kogălniceanu. The Jews would then enjoy the same opportunities and guarantees that, for example, Bulgarians or Armenians did. For this reason he saw no danger in allowing the naturalization of the approximately one thousand Jews which accompanied the revision of Article 7 of the constitution. Again, the foreign minister occasionally lapsed into inconsistency in describing the dilemma posed by this immigrant population. Here his anti-Semitism took a statistical approach. In other situations he emphasized the lack of cultural assimilation, insisting that the Jews could not become citizens until they embraced Romanian sentiments and customs. Characteristic of Kogălniceanu and the broad spectrum of Romanian anti-Jewish sentiment, then, was an ad hoc style of argumentation; namely, use whatever serves the national purpose at this point.[14]

Perhaps, Kogălniceanu's anti-Semitic attitudes best displayed themselves in a series of observations made in the legislature during March of 1879. At this juncture, in the midst of "Jewish jokes," references to Moldavia as a "new Jerusalem," and repeated use of variants of "Yid," he spelled out his tactics to deal with the Great Powers and the volatile internal situation. Whereas he had been careful and modulated when theorizing about tolerance for other Christian sects, he resonated a good deal more aggressively in this arena. Six months prior to this debate Kogălniceanu had been far more adamant on the issue of Bessarabia's loss, hardly mentioning the issue of minority rights, but now "the Jewish question is more grave than that

---

[14] Kogălniceanu, *Opere*, IV, 63, 147, & 179.

of Bessarabia." Exhibiting much more fervor as an anti-Semite Kogălniceanu repeated the charges relating to foreign intervention in the domestic affairs of the country, the humiliation suffered by the Romanian people, and the unacceptably large number of Jews then living in the northern province, but then he distinguished himself and the tradition of Romanian anti-Semitism we are discussing from the more extremist varieties. Though by no means in a benevolent category, his stand rejected the systematic use of force as a standard governmental instrument and specifically any attempt at extermination. In the effort to preserve Romanian, especially Moldavian, individuality the anti-Semitic heritage represented by Kogălniceanu advocated a utilitarian employment of the Jews. Hardly idealistic, but over the next three generations perceiving the Jewish community as somehow being "useful" would make a critical difference in its chances of survival. Finally, in the spring of 1879 neither Kogălniceanu nor the delegates to whom he spoke had any intention of permitting a revised Article 7 to precipitate major changes in Romanian society. For this reason they fought doggedly to avoid sweeping categories of Jews eligible for naturalization under the guidelines of the Congress of Berlin. Other than the token emancipation of the circa one thousand veterans, which everyone considered an exceptional act for public relations purposes and not to be repeated, there would be no en bloc naturalizations. Kogălniceanu maintained that a literal execution of Article XLIV and full equality for the Jews in Romania meant social revolution. He, therefore, lectured the delegates on the national danger this constituted and equated patriotism with the denial of full enfranchisement for the Jews. Kogălniceanu's stance on tolerance altered dramatically, then, when he faced what he termed the prospect of "a radical transformation in all the circumstances of the country." He would see that Article 7 was revised and carried out in such a manner as to preclude basic changes for the Romanians or the Jews.[15]

In the fall just before the compromise allowing for the revision of Article 7 was worked out, Kogălniceanu refined his presentation on the Jewish issue yet further. Though persisting in dwelling on the themes of foreign intervention and national

---

[15] Ibid., 637; Kogălniceanu, *Opere*, V, 73–5 & 79–84; Verax [Radu Rosetti], *La Roumanie et les Juifs* (Bucarest: I. V. Socecu, 1903), 167.

humiliation, he rejected as a matter of policy all rationalizations for widespread violence against the Jewish community. On the issue of what would in the next century be known as genocide, Kogălniceanu objected to mass slaughter as not fitting for a modern European country of the nineteenth century. To the suggestion that the Jews be driven out of Romania Kogălniceanu's response was to the point and practical: Romania had not had in times past and did not currently possess the ability to stem such immigration. The nation would have similar luck in attempting to expel several hundred thousand Jews from the country. Once more the analysis proceeded matter of factly and in a nonaltruistic manner. His concern centered on what was best for the country, though this might also be beneficial for the Jewish community. Keeping in mind that he repudiated general emancipation and subscribed to bureaucratic impediments to naturalization, we must acknowledge that he advocated making friends, not enemies, of Romanian Jews. In this fashion they might be useful to the nation and its progress. Recognizing as Kogălniceanu put it that there was "no deliverance from the Jews," the Romanians should try to assimilate them. As we will be seeing in greater detail later, the type of assimilation envisaged in the Romanian anti-Semitic tradition ruled out force on theoretical grounds, but it did call for the disappearance of the Jewish community as an identifiable group. Tolerance would not have been necessary, since the nation would have become absolutely homogeneous. Kogălniceanu thought that only in this fashion could the nation protect its threatened province along the Russian border as well as its most essential socioeconomic interests.[16]

Unhappily the foreign minister's elaboration of the Jewish question did not end on quite this much of a generous note. The marked xenophobic trait emerged again in a reaction against the political and press activities of the Alliance Israélite. This agency's endeavors, seen by the Romanians as foreign interference in their private affairs, stirred up enormous enmity against the Jews and the entire issue of equality of rights. Kogălniceanu rationalized a policy combining nonviolence with limited access to naturalization for the Jews. But he also pan-

---

[16] Kogălniceanu, *Opere*, V, 134–6 & 177.

dered to the more bigoted anti-Semites by proclaiming the Alliance Israélite the greatest "enemy" of Romanian Jews. To great applause he pronounced that that organization had done more harm to the interests of Romanian Jewry than any other group. Though the logic is not impeccable he later continued on to make the point that the Alliance Israélite also represented the principal enemy of the Romanian nation and its basic interests. This line of thought produced a veiled threat that the Alliance Israélite's activities and the identification of the Romanian Jewish community with that organization foretold significant hindrances to additional naturalizations. Kogălniceanu's prophecy was both accurate and an encouragement to that end. The nationalistic and anti-Semitic backlash between 1880 and 1914 fulfilled his conviction and intent.[17]

Active in the independence crisis of 1877–1880 along with Kogălniceanu, Titu Liviu Maiorescu (1840–1917) enjoyed a career spanning the entire period under discussion. Politician, historian, man of letters, and one of Romania's most outstanding literary critics, Maiorescu represented a pinnacle in Romanian cultural growth. His influence throughout the late nineteenth and early twentieth centuries was substantial by any calculation. This impact continues today in the reprinting of his works as well as in the reading they receive by the intellectual elite and in the educational system. That such a man should also be a committed and articulate anti-Semite constitutes another major factor in the evolution of a system of rationalized bias that contains unique components and emphases. The fact that men of this caliber endorsed anti-Semitic concepts, expressing them in a piquing way, gave that assessment of the Jewish community a prevalence and cachet not usually associated with it in the Western world. The affiliation of a Maiorescu with anti-Semitism helped establish in the minds of the intelligentsia and ruling elements in Romanian society an instinctive link between nationalism and this prejudice. But for Maiorescu this association remained carefully articulated and more moderate than that of many of his Moldavian compatriots. As leader of the literary movement known as *Junimea* ("The Youth"),

---

[17] Eugen Weber, "Romania," in *The European Right*, Hans Rogger & Eugen Weber (eds.), (Berkeley & Los Angeles: University of California Press, 1966), 506; Kogălniceanu, *Opere*, V, 171 & 179.

Maiorescu never endorsed the chauvinistic pretenses of some of his contemporaries. His nationalism, whether expressed in the cultural or political fora, reflected his broader exposure to Western culture (especially through travel and education in Germany). Not uncritical of certain strains of Romanian nationalism Maiorescu and the Junamists fought against the cultural, literary, and political exaggerations of the chauvinists. Subjecting the Principalities' history to a more modern and objective scrutiny Maiorescu strove for a detailed, unbiased understanding of his nation's past so as to determine better current political policies. By contemporary Romanian standards, then, he represented a broadminded, reformist trend in political as well as intellectual matters. Most germanely here Maiorescu rejected the extreme opinions of the "false nationalists." He brought to the intelligentsia a level of education and breadth of culture not present before. Because of these attributes, he and his circle dominated Romanian thought in the period from Prince Carol's ascension to the throne in 1866 until shortly after the proclamation of the Kingdom of Romania in 1881.[18]

Maiorescu's approach to the Jewish question in Romania, while being no less anti-Semitic at its core, took on a similar sophistication in comparison to the more usual and blatant variants then rampant. His starting point consisted of the observation that the fundamental problem was not the impact of foreigners (especially Jews), but rather the deplorable level of education and economic activity among Romanians. In fact Romanian society needed and would continue to require the assistance of the Jews. Until the native population began to supply the resources and services currently provided by strangers, Romania could not dispense with its Jewish community. That this condition was unwelcome and unwise Maiorescu conceded. However, he also emphasized that to attack the Jews simply wasted time and the national resources to the conspicuous detriment of the Romanian state. Persecution, and certainly violence of any sort, would merely unleash barbarism and ignorance where more intelligent activity was so desperately demanded.[19] Concurring with the utilitarian

---

18 Bénédict Kanner, *La Société Littéraire Junimea de Iassy et son Influence sur Le Mouvement Intellectuel en Roumanie* (Paris: Bonvalot-Jouve, 1906), 37, 61–6, & 229–31.

19 Titu Maiorescu, *Critice*, II. Domnica Filimon-Stoicescu (ed.), (București: Editura pentru Literatură, 1967), 205.

theme that made up such an essential part of Romanian anti-Semitism, Maiorescu contended that the Jews could not be removed from contemporary Romania. Only when the Romanians could assume the Jewish role in the economy, and perhaps not even then, could the Danubian state consider ridding itself of this group. As a matter of fact, he likewise argued against expulsion on the more idealistic grounds of humanitarian sentiment and political liberalism. However, he did tailor his outlook more to the prevailing nationalistic temper during the constitutional crisis of 1878–1880. But when not engrossed in the heat of battle, Maiorescu took the stand that these fundamentals of liberalism and humanitarianism should not be circumvented under any pretext. Even during the debates of the constituent assembly Maiorescu saw himself as standing between the two extremes of complete rejection of the Jews and uncritical acceptance of them into the body politic en masse. He would not expel them nor did he believe ethnic hatred had any role to play in this equation. The emphasis he wished to pursue dictated the conservation of the nation's base, whether cultural, economic, or ethnic. Romania needed a national evolution to a higher plane of culture and commercial activity, not pogroms.[20]

Maiorescu's moderate anti-Semitism was such, therefore, that he saw—and somewhat quixotically proclaimed—himself not to be an enemy of the Jews. He combatted intellectually the more extreme anti-Semites then prominent in Romanian cultural and political life. At least in the case of the assimilated Jew he spoke for the values of nineteenth century liberal civilization and tolerance. A sign of the times can be found in the fact that Maiorescu had to contend during these parliamentary debates with the politically damaging accusation of being a "friend of the Jews." While acknowledging the absence of any personal antipathy towards the Jewish community, he attempted to defuse this indictment. He responded that he was a friend of the Jews in the exact same sense that he was a friend of all congeries drawn from "foreign nations." During the process of revising Article 7, in some limited sense he called

[20] E. Lovinescu, *T. Maiorescu*, I (1840–1876). (București: Fundația pentru Literatură și Artă "Regele Carol II," 1940), 256–7; E. Lovinescu, *T. Maiorescu*, II (1876–1917). (București: Fundația pentru Literatură și Artă "Regele Carol II," 1940), 50–1.

for a more humane spirit and some compromise. He specified an approach that placed him behind the movement for Jewish rights in the same degree that he would be for those of any other group of alien nationals. But once more the appraisal remained largely utilitarian. For this analysis did not automatically rule out what the outside observer might label discriminatory treatment. If the national exigencies of Romania called for it, Maiorescu left himself an opening to treat any foreigner (Jew or otherwise) evenhandedly but in a prejudicial fashion. The crucial factor according to his vision, though, should not be religion or Jewishness. Like every other Romanian patriot he sought above all else to protect the nation and its traditions. Maiorescu simply defined these, along with the best means of protecting them, in a different fashion than did the chauvinist. He did not necessarily rule out arbitrary and capricious handling of minorities. Rather he thought that the Jews should not be the exclusive object of this type of treatment.[21]

A man of less provincial views than most of his contemporaries, Maiorescu also manifested considerably more in the way of humanitarian sentiment. Willing to analyze coolly Romanian society and propose reformist ideas based on his observations of other cultures, he too drew the line with the conservation of Romania's national heritage. He saw the naturalization issue as the beginning not the end of the Jewish question in Romania. Consequently Maiorescu professed categorically anti-Semitic opinions during the course of the constitutional debates of the late 1870s. He perceived the number of Jews in Romania as being alarmingly great by the end of the Congress of Berlin. With the naturalization decision signifying that this population might become a permanent part of daily life in the new state, he expressed alarm over the possibility of preserving the character of Romanian national life. His motivation in departing from previously annunciated humanitarian convictions regarding equal rights for the Jews centered on what he described as "a justified partiality in favor of national values." He wanted guarantees that relaxed criteria for naturalization would not produce an influx of Jewish citizens

---

[21] Titu Maiorescu, *Discursuri parlamentare*, II (1876–1881), (Bucureşti: Editura Librăriei Socecŭ & Comp., 1897), 337 & 366.

which would alter Romanian traditions. What the native Romanian wanted to be, how he wished to remain unique in his ethnicity, took precedence over more libertarian concepts.[22] During the heated discussions of the constituent assembly, then, Maiorescu objected to a perceived foreign intrusion into Romania's domestic affairs. Outsiders, whether Jewish or gentile, had no business meddling in the constitutional order of the Danubian state. The fact that both the Great Powers and the Alliance Israélite had done so constituted a blow to Romania's national dignity. As with others in the constituent assembly, he predicted that this pressure from without would redound to the Jews' discredit. If Bucharest had been left alone, Maiorescu claimed the matter of minority rights might have been worked out in a spirit of "peaceful humaneness." Since this had not been the case, he hinted quite strongly that there existed a sentiment of revolt in the country against this unacceptable pressure. If legislators like himself had at one time considered extending equal rights to the Jewish community, Maiorescu now stressed that the aggressive – even imprudent – tactics employed by foreigners had made this impossible. He and his peers were accordingly compelled to revert to a more defensive mentality. Maiorescu underscored how they should protect Romanian interests above all else.[23]

Maiorescu's anti-Semitism and his political stance in the constituent assembly culminated in his advice to accept the dictates of the Congress of Berlin. He amplified this conviction to include the wile of rendering them void through interpretation. From his point of view, the religious intolerance of Article 7 of the Romanian constitution amounted to an anachronism in any case. Even before the 1877–1878 war annulled Muslim Ottoman sovereignty over the Danubian Principalities, the real points at issue for his country could not be subsumed within the confines of sectarian squabbles. Maiorescu declared the country's fate much more embroiled with the spread of Western culture and the impact of the concept of nationality. He saw Romania's status as a "Latin nation" as possessing greater moment than the fact that a majority of the population followed

---

[22] Kanner, *La Société Littéraire Junimea*, 255; Maiorescu, *Discursuri parlamentare*, II, 368 & 374–89.

[23] Maiorescu, *Discursuri parlamentare*, II, 198–200, 250–1, & 367.

the rites of the Eastern Orthodox branch of Christianity. In the modern era only the more backward states such as Russia still embraced a sense of religious exclusivity or mission according to Maiorescu. As a Latin nation faced not only with an internal minorities problem but also surrounded by "a wilderness of other races," Romania's differentiating traits had to be those of blood, language, and a common culture. Religion as a part of the national profile Maiorescu relegated to a secondary role. It served as no more than an accessory to the truly essential aspects of nationality. Restrictions based on religious norms should therefore be removed from the constitution. They had no place there for both theoretical and practical reasons. In great part these standard anti-Semitic disabilities based on religion no longer served the purposes of Romania in a nationalistic era. Maiorescu did not believe that restrictions on the Jewish community had become unnecessary, but simply that different ones would be more opportune and effective at this juncture. The challenge for the new Romania resided in devising anti-Jewish disabilities more "in consonance with contemporary views"; namely, restrictions that could be explained away in nineteenth century terms acceptable to the liberal states of Western Europe. In place of religious handicaps as impediments to naturalization he advocated any and all economic or social constraints on the Jews. These would be more appropriate as well as less likely to occasion the type of public relations gaffe which allowed the Alliance Israélite to galvanize the Great Powers against Romania. Finally, Maiorescu emphasized the critical import of enabling legislation. As long as Bucharest retained the right under the revised constitution to decide how equality of rights should be implemented, then the national culture remained safe. The key proviso (i.e., whether the Jewish community obtained the constitutional right to be naturalized through categories, lists, or individually) continued to be the Romanians' ability to construe what Article XLIV of Berlin meant in practice. As Maiorescu bluntly put it, no agency—Great Power or Alliance Israélite—would be in a position to project itself into the details of domestic legislation or administration. In Romania no foreigner would be able to insure the execution of the Jews' newly won equality. As long as Maiorescu's compatriots removed the glaringly inept manifestations of religious intolerance from their constitution, he assured his countrymen that they would be able to prescribe the outcome of the Jewish issue. They would still have the power to protect their nation as they best saw fit. In the end Maiorescu proclaimed the matter of Jewish rights in Romania, even under the strictures of Berlin, to be "a question of judgment and . . . in this case [i.e., Jewish rights] which directly affects our national interest we will make that judgment so as to conserve our nationality." Thus disingenuousness became both a standard part of Romanian anti-Semitism and a useful stratagem in the successful bid to obtain the recognition of Europe.[24]

If Kogălniceanu and Maiorescu represented the comparatively moderate wing of Romanian anti-Semitism, Mihai Eminescu (1850–1889) stood out as the most eloquent spokesman of the radical anti-Semites. Yet another Moldavian, Eminescu exhibited in both the artistic and political realms the behavior of an extraordinarily enthusiastic nationalist. A romantic in his creative writing, he displayed the same tendencies and temperament when confronted with the volatile issue of Jewish rights. He insisted that national politics as well as art reflect the popular base to be found in the Romanian ethnic tradition.[25] Bureaucrat, educator, junior level diplomat, library director, and journalist, Eminescu achieved his lasting and profound impact on Romanian culture as a poet. From mid-nineteenth century to the present his influence as the national poet of Romania has remained immense. His impact as a literary figure as well as an advocate of a rabid nationalism shaped the intelligentsia from the time of the independence crisis of the late 1870s to the present day. If any one summed up the identification between anti-Semitism and the core of Romanian culture, it was Eminescu. As the paramount and most influential writer in the Romanian language, their Shakespeare in terms of towering presence and pervading cultural legend, he legitimized bias against the Jews. His legacy in this forum as well as in that of letters has made itself felt across the spectrum of nationalistic intellectuals for the last hundred years.[26]

In Eminescu we find ourselves depicting an apostle of ethnic nationalism, one whose works appeared not only on the shelves

---

[24] Ibid., 281–3, 287, & 365; Lovinescu, *T. Maiorescu*, 50–1.
[25] Lovinescu, *T. Maiorescu*, 50; Kanner, *La Société Littéraire Junimea*, 182–3 & 187.
[26] Eugen Weber, "Romania," 507; Kanner, *La Société Littéraire Junimea*, 188.

of the intelligentsia but also in the curricula of all schools and universities. The Western reader unacquainted with Eastern Europe will have to imagine a situation in which the preeminent literary figure of a nation embraced racial prejudice. In doing so this verbal artiste lent it the full weight of his reputation. Perhaps, Eminescu's influence as littérateur and anti-Semite found its fulsome expression in the dust jacket advertisement of the edition of his political works that appeared early in World War II. This two-volume anthology was touted in the following language: "Behold the true patriotism! Here is the gospel of Romanian nationalism!" A substantial portion of that "gospel" dealt with Eminescu's evaluation of the Jewish community in Romania and his subsequent anti-Semitism founded on that assessment. To gauge the impact of the ideas we will now analyze, we must keep in mind his central position in Romanian intellectual history. In addition this consideration will illustrate the ethical vulnerability of even the most rarefied of intellectual environments. We must accept the fact that otherwise unexpected, seemingly incongruous factors like anti-Semitism can find there both a home and a startling appeal.[27]

For Eminescu the ultimate value in life, indeed he identified it as the "supreme law," consisted in the preservation of country and nationality. He went so far as to maintain that nation and people possessed such transcendent worth that any course of action could be justified in their defense. He specifically rejected nineteenth century Western notions of civilization and humanitarianism. These might occasion risk for the national traditions. As a singularly intractable ethnic enthusiast, he relegated all other qualities and predispositions to a second order of importance. Individuals, events, and facts possessed enough significance to be taken into account insofar as they contributed to the new state's interest. For the committed patriot the patria had to be the overriding preoccupation. Since that polity formed the core of reality in Eminescu's estimation, the nationalist was not simply permitted but required to protect it by any means suitable. This imperative held true even at the cost

---

[27] "Iată adevăratul patriotism! Iată evanghelia naţionalismului românesc!"; see Mihail Eminescu, *Opera politică*, I (1870–1879) & II (1880–1883), I. Creţu (ed.), (Bucureşti: Cugetarea—Georgescu Delafras, 1941).

of damage to one's humaneness or integrity (as one native interpreter of Eminescu put it, safeguarding the country "through duplicity and Byzantine cunning"). In the end, the nation assumed such moment as the creative force behind all civilization that Eminescu believed its values must determine all political and cultural policies.[28] Like many other nationalists he elaborated long lists of characteristics deemed essential aspects of his country's nationalism. Often times these grew as much out of a repudiation of the minority's lineaments (especially those of the Jews) as out of a positive summary of Romanian attributes.[29] Eminescu's basic commitment to Romania rested on the conviction that unless the country remained "national" (namely, possessed of a unique character delimited by the Romanian ethnic element) then it did not deserve to exist. Obviously there could be no other reason for there to be a Kingdom of Romania than to be a national homeland. Therefore the inherent nature or genius of the Romanians had to take precedence over the rights of other groups resident in the country. In speaking of the Jewish issue after independence and the theoretical granting of equality, Eminescu declared that "either this country will be truly Romanian or it does not merit to be." The acceptance of Article XLIV of the Congress of Berlin had settled nothing in the mind of Romania's most distinguished author and anti-Semite.[30]

Before and after the attainment of national independence, Eminescu persisted in seeing the status as well as the aspirations of the Jewish community as clashing with the well-being of Romania. What already existed and certainly any enhancement of Jewish rights posed more than a theoretical problem for the country. They amounted in a very real sense to "a question of life and death." Slipping into the same use of epithets that we encountered with Kogălniceanu, he expressed alarm at the large numbers of Jews who might become a burden upon the state. In his evaluation they presently constituted a danger to the Romanian nationality, when they did not possess equality of rights. They would be so much the more a peril once naturalized to any extent. Eminescu allowed himself only the slightest

---

[28] Eminescu, *Opera politica*, I, 472; Murărasu, *Naţionalismul lui Eminescu*, 299 & 352.
[29] Murărasu, *Naţionalismul lui Eminescu*, 226–7.
[30] Ibid., 153 & 253.

of qualifications on this generalization. "A limited number of useful Jews" might be discovered intermixed with "the hundreds of thousands of nonproductive and alien intruders."[31] In the public debate and turmoil over the revision of Article 7 of the Romanian constitution, then, Eminescu stressed the enormity of the sacrifice demanded by the Congress of Berlin. The culture of mid-nineteenth century Romania he described as already debased and weakened. It could not withstand the impact of emancipated Jews in large numbers. Eminescu claimed that wherever in Europe the Jewish community had been awarded the rights of citizenship, there it had "falsified and corrupted the native culture." He acknowledged that the religious discrimination of Article 7 did occasionally constitute a defect. Some small percentage of the Jews in Romania merited the rights of citizenship, though the multitude did not. This injustice he said should be rectified with or without the pressure of an Article XLIV. He went so far in his rationalization as to claim that amelioration would be accomplished for purely humanitarian reasons and in the absence of foreign intervention. As in many components of the anti-Semitic tradition created by Eminescu and the other intellectuals we are considering, an element of ad hoc inconsistency occurs at this point. The fabric of this prejudice is not of a whole cloth and is meant to cover whatever challenges happen to materialize at a given moment.[32]

An example of this discrepancy in anti-Semitic argumentation can be found in the question of whether or not a Jew can be a Romanian. Eminescu's more usual position stated that native Jews existed nowhere in Europe. For him, ". . . the Jews are not—cannot be Romanians, as in general they are not and cannot be German, English, French, Italian." The Jews in Romania comprised a foreign invasion, therefore, because they did not have Romanian as their maternal tongue or adopt the native customs. Too conscious of their own racial identity, Eminescu saw the Jews as unwilling to commit themselves to and take pride in being Romanian. These cultural differences he characterized both in terms of being alien and inimical to the national interest. But on other occasions, while continuing to

---

[31] Eminescu, *Opera politica*, I, 97–8; Murărasu, *Naţionalismul*, 149–50.
[32] Eminescu, *Opera politica*, I, 487 & 498.

maintain that there were no Romanian Jews just foreign ones resident in the country, he indicated that German, Spanish, Polish, and other varieties did exist. Perhaps, the explanation lies in the sense of rejection he felt, of Romanian culture not being perceived as worthy of the effort of adoption. This ethnically hostile group had accommodated itself to other cultures by speaking the native languages and picking up the rudiments of various sets of national usages. But the Jews did not do so in Romania.[33] In the same vein, Eminescu demanded that the Jewish community in Romania assimilate, if it wished to obtain equal rights. At the same time he denied that assimilation could be achieved. In his equivocation on this point, he seems to have been disturbed on two different levels. First, he did not want to see the native Romanian culture adulterated or destroyed by the "pathological" impact of the Jews. Second, he thought the Romanians did not possess the requisite economic skills to compete with this community. In both areas he believed that because of Jewish ability and Romanian heedlessness the national organism would be absorbed, if not destroyed. Committed nationalists had to protect it from the more vigorous Jewish element. This process of disintegration in native cultures, according to his views, had been the usual one. Whether the Jews enjoyed the rights of an emancipated citizenry or remained restricted by certain disabilities as in Romania they threatened the national mores. Whatever the local conditions, Eminescu proclaimed that "they are Jews and cannot be anything else."[34]

Eminescu's ambivalent attitude towards Jewish assimilation, then, emphasized Romanian as well as Jewish shortcomings. The basis for the "Jewish question" in Romania he defined as the economic backwardness and lack of appropriate attitudes on the part of the Romanians themselves. He saw his countrymen as lacking in initiative and any entrepreneurial drive. Instead of being motivated by a spirit of individual success and national foresight, he thought most literate Romanians preferred feeding off the national treasury as bureaucrats. In addition, but for the agrarian problem and the abominable condition of the vast majority of Romanians who were peas-

---

[33] Ibid., 105; Murărasu, *Naționalismul*, 147.
[34] Eminescu, *Opera politica*, I, 539 & 545–6; Murărasu, *Naționalismul*, 148–9.

ants he said there would not be a "Jewish problem." Create a strong, enterprising class of peasant proprietors and the question of the Jews in Romania would resolve itself.[35] Obviously, as one of the most outspoken of Romanian anti-Semites, Eminescu placed more accent on the Jewish side of the equation. He began by stressing the quality of "social corruption." The Jewish community in his view represented a marked case, since they did not value work as the creative force which ultimately gave individuals political rights. The Jews were, rather, an economic army dealing with foreigners to the detriment of Romanian values. Whether or not they had equal political rights, according to Eminescu they always conducted themselves as Jews, not as natives would. They were unscrupulous egoists who wanted full rights of citizenship without demonstrating a corresponding desire to sacrifice for and serve the Romanian nation. Eminescu saw the Jews only as consumers of the country's wealth and not as contributors to the national welfare. The Jews became in his estimation the single group in the country attempting to obtain the rights of citizenship without participating in the hard work of creating the new state. Their presence in the country amounted to "the symptom of a social disease, a crisis in the life of the [Romanian] people. . . ." If this "extraordinarily greedy, unscrupulous, and inhumane" element were not restrained in some fashion, Eminescu believed it would dominate and exploit the rural population. Finally, the Jewish community constituted both in itself and through its use of foreign intermediaries to obtain otherwise inaccessible rights a deleterious influence on Romanian culture. Autochthonous values and populations could not in Eminescu's worldview survive, if free play were to be given to the undesirable activities of a group like the Jews.[36]

In approaching a definitive statement on the Jewish issue, Eminescu took as his starting point the view that the Romanian element in the state must remain the dominant one. As the epitome of nineteenth century nationalism in Romania, he specified that its culture, history and ethnic characteristics had to set the pattern for the state's development. He most emphatically rejected any immigration policies and possibil-

---

[35] Eminescu, *Opera politica*, I, 417; Murărasu, *Naţionalismul*, 149 & 151.
[36] Eminescu, *Opera politica*, I, 100–1, 108, 417; Murărasu, *Naţionalismul*, 146 & 258.

ities of naturalization for the Jews that might produce what he disparagingly termed the cosmopolitan opposite of a national state; namely, an "America of the Danube." According to his most prominent Romanian critic, Eminescu preached not an East European version of patriotic supremacy, but rather "an ethic of nationalism." The goal here became a continued national existence stressing the creative factors in the country, not an aggression directed against others.[37] More of a xenophobe than a physically violent fanatic then, Eminescu preached against foreign influences whether these came by way of the Jews or through the aristocracy's borrowings from the culture of Western Europe. In the case of the Jews, however, he affected to believe that their sense of racial consciousness was so great as to preclude any sense of identity with Romanians. They became by his definition cosmopolitan and part of an international alliance designed to engineer a public relations tumult proving that they were persecuted. In his opinion the whole Jewish question remained a phony one, simply a "pretext" for foreigners to intervene in an unwarranted fashion in the domestic affairs of the country. And as such Eminescu resented it bitterly. The Jews of Romania were for him foreigners and enemies. They would remain in these categories until they learned Romanian ways, especially the native language, and broke their ties with outsiders. Like most other anti-Semites Eminescu indicated that they would regret having occasioned foreign intervention in the form of Article XLIV of the Congress of Berlin.[38]

In the end Eminescu backed the use of nonviolent, legal restrictions on Jewish access to equal rights. Rejecting persecutions and other conspicuously overt manifestations of hatred, he supported an approach indicative of a national instinct of preservation exclusive of religious norms. He continued to vacillate on whether or not a few Jews might assimilate and prove useful to the nation. He went along, however, with those who used this argument for political purposes. Despite his depiction of the failings of Romanian society he also persisted in his more extreme moments in accusing the Jews of caus-

---

[37] Eminescu, *Opera politica*, II, 389; Murărasu, *Naţionalismul*, 309, 349, & 351.
[38] Eminescu, *Opera politica*, I, 507, 518–20, & 522–3; Murărasu, *Naţionalismul*, 147–8 & 153.

ing the major moral lapses in the Romanian character. Or as Eminescu put it, "The Romanian is lazy, immoral, vicious. Why however is he not immoral or vicious where there are no Jews [sic]?" Thus, when the revised edition of Article 7 of the Romanian constitution emerged from the constituent assembly he did more than trumpet the fact that it met the exigencies of Berlin. He believed, and publicly said as much for the benefit of the disconsolate and inveterate anti-Semites, that they had won. In that document Eminescu had his non-violent, secular means of continuing to exclude the bulk of Romania's Jews from equal rights. They remained isolated from any real opportunity to become citizens. For Eminescu they likewise retained the status of nonRomanians in culture, history, and aspirations.[39]

On a different but still interesting level of influence on Romanian culture and anti-Semitism we find Bogdan Petriceicu Hasdeu (1838–1907). Born in Hotin in what is now the Moldavian S.S.R. and what the Romanian nationalist continues to refer to as the province of Bessarabia, Hasdeu stood out as the first Romanian historian to write a national history based on the systematic use of documentary research. His historical writings brought a new depth of historical analysis as well as increased psychological insight to the study of Romanian history. Deserting from the "Count Radetzky" cavalry regiment after his service in the Russian army during the Crimean War, he emigrated to the Danubian Principalities in 1856 becoming a determined advocate for the national cause. Though a pioneer in his historical writings, Hasdeu did not achieve the stature or have the impact of the other anti-Semites we are studying. He passes muster among Romania's savants, however, because of his encyclopedic learning, especially in the field of linguistics.[40] An intellectual opponent of Maiorescu and Eminescu, Hasdeu closely approximated the blind nationalism which these leaders of the Junimea movement resisted. His fixation upon things Romanian often times excluded a broader view of culture and history. Though his main interest centered on Roma-

---

[39] Eminescu, *Opera politica*, I, 97–8, 100–3, 418–9 & 545–6; Eminescu, *Opera politica*, II, 370; Murărasu, *Naționalismul*, 152.

[40] Marin Ştefănescu, *Filosofia Românească* (Bucureşti: Institutul de Arte Grafice "Răsăritul," 1922), 145–6; Kanner, *La Société Littéraire Junimea,* 225–7.

FIGURE VI. Bogdan Petriceicu Hasdeu. From: *B. P. Hasdeu* by Mihai Drăgan, Editura Junimea, 1972.

nian history, he also labored as a professor, journalist, university librarian, archivist, a member of the literati, and a linguist of extraordinary capabilities. A polymath in his teaching as well as his research interests, Hasdeu served as an instructor in subjects as diverse as history and languages on the one hand and statistics and geography on the other. In later life his cultural influence could also be seen in his activity as a functionary of the Romanian Academy as well as the recipient of one of its most important awards.[41]

---

[41] Kanner, *La Société*, 229–31; L. Marian, *Bogdan Petriceicu Hasdeu* (București: "Cartea Româneasca," 1928), 3–6 & 16–7.

In understanding Hasdeu's anti-Semitism we must be aware of his profound indoctrination as a Romanian and a Christian. Those who did not belong to these two groups he immediately and automatically classified as enemies. Along this line Hasdeu became a devotee of spiritualism, seemingly believing that at times he could communicate with the preternatural. Whatever his personal beliefs, he placed significant emphasis upon the broad tradition of Eastern Orthodoxy among the Romanian people. This metaphysics informed both his philosophy of history and his theory of nationalism.[42]

In gauging the thrust and rigor of Hasdeu's anti-Semitism perhaps the best place to begin would be with his labeling of the moderates' efforts during the debate over Jewish rights. He stood out as the one who accused Kogălniceanu of being guilty of "filosemitism" for his more temperate version of Romanian anti-Jewish sentiment. A decade before the Congress of Berlin and its demands for constitutional revision, Hasdeu declaimed upon the "invasion" of Romania by the Jews. As early as 1868, then, he called for a vigorous nationalism which would serve as a "political religion" for the nation. The purpose of this religious patriotism would be "to combat energetically the spread and deceit of Judaism."[43] As with so many of the anti-Semitic intelligentsia he quickly countered that some of his best friends were Jewish. Interestingly though, as we shall discuss in more detail in the next chapter, rarely did a Romanian Jew possess enough "culture" to qualify for his friendship. The more likely recipients of this accolade were foreign Jews educated according to Western norms. The basis of the argument resided not simply in his own inherent anti-Semitism, but in his contention that all Romanians were anti-Semites. To have incorporated the national traditions and Orthodoxy into one's personality meant that every Romanian, not only the extreme nationalist, had to be motivated by anti-Semitic attitudes. For Hasdeu the status of being a nationalist and a nineteenth century democrat carried with it the corollary of a fierce anti-Jewish mission. Despite being a convinced republican where domestic economic and political factors came into play (that is, on all issues except the Jewish), he obviously

---

[42] Marin, *Hasdeu*, 4–5, Ştefănescu, *Filisofia Românească*, 146–9 & 151.
[43] Hasdeu, *Scrieri Literare, Morale, şi Politice*, 331–2.

stressed the nationalist concerns over the libertarian in the latter instance. On the Jewish question he reversed his political affinities, joining the conservatives and abandoning former compatriots like Kogălniceanu. The ethnic and religious values overpowered his otherwise liberal goals.[44]

As both a prolific publicist and highly visible activist Hasdeu comported himself as an extreme xenophobe, one who specialized in anti-Semitic rhetoric. In these roles he also added unusual aspects to the substance and tenor of Romanian anti-Semitism. First, he borrowed for Romanian nationalistic purposes the Western philosophical concept of "providence" which appears in the title of this study. Though employing it in a more benevolent and less fortuitous sense than his Western source, Hasdeu clearly linked the notion of providential intervention with the fate of the nation. He specifically identified it with the entirety of the territory traditionally claimed by the extreme Romanian nationalists. The Jews could not claim to have been included in this "providential selection" by God and nature, one that had constituted the Romanian people and their incipient independent state. They had to remain excluded from participation in the nation by their very essence. And Hasdeu's nationalism allowed for no compromise on this point.[45] Second, he provided a unique contribution to the Romanian anti-Semite's notion of assimilation and its possibilities. According to him only Jewish men posed a threat to the Romanian nation and its future. Reflecting his Jewish grandmother's sway, Hasdeu maintained that Jewish women did not constitute a danger to nationalistic values because they "remain feminine" and "do not study the Talmud." Unfortunately he did not elaborate on the matters of quality and culture in this regard. Most likely even Jewish women remained acceptable only insofar as they manifested upperclass and refined cultural inclinations. In any case they did not represent as men might the cosmopolitan and foreign influences which radical nationalists and fervid anti-Semites feared.[46]

Whereas Hasdeu evolved his anti-Semitism briefly and to

---

[44] Ibid., 333–4; Marin, *Hasdeu*, 8–9.
[45] Marian, *Hasdeu*, 10; B. P. Hasdeu, *Istoria Critica a Romaniloru*, II (Bucuresci: Typographia Antoniu Manescu, 1874), 10.
[46] Hasdeu, *Scrieri Literare*, 335; Kanner, *La Société*, 62–3.

FIGURE VII. Alexandru D. Xenopol. From: *A. D. Xenopol*, in *Editura Enciclo-pedică Română.*

the point, Alexandru D. Xenopol (1847–1920) developed his complex variety at greater length. A native of Iaşi with its large, recently immigrated Jewish population, he worked initially as a magistrate and lawyer. Only later did he settle into his voca-tion as a historian of the Romanian nation. In this capacity he achieved marked success. He became not only the rector of the University of Iaşi but also a luminary in the Romanian

Academy and an honorary professor at the Sorbonne. As an intellectual and a patriot Xenopol demonstrated in his prolix writing the conviction that only through nationalism could one become a true humanitarian. His constellation of ideas included in its hierarchy, then, the preeminence of the Romanian nation as a powerful force impelling the evolution of the individual and the progress of mankind. Only in this context could an individual find happiness and contribute towards either the common good or the continued development of humanity. Declaring that there was no such thing as humankind in the abstract, Xenopol posited that men exist only in the form given them by their nationality. The Romanian people, therefore, must have a distinctively national life as well as a mature self-awareness of themselves as ethnically-culturally unique. Only through protecting these qualities did Xenopol think the Romanians could endow mankind with anything of interest and suitable for historical remembrance.[47]

In Xenopol's mind peoples, just as individuals, possessed a natural tendency to defend and deepen their individuality. This national orientation, however, had to become a part of the fabric of the governing classes. Only insofar as the intelligentsia and the governmental groups trained and influenced by it incorporated this mentality into their policies would it be possible to arrive at a "*rational* nationalism" (emphasis in the original). Such a rational nationalism became, in his view, the sole guarantee of the Romanian people's survival and growth. Accordingly, he saw anti-Semitism as a basic characteristic of Romanian nationalism. He took this prejudice so much for granted as a fundamental of political life that he maintained that it was impossible to distinguish among parties on this basis. Xenopol simply presumed that any educated Romanian, whatever his class origins, had to display anti-Semitic traits. In a similar manner any Romanian political party would have as an essential portion of its program this anti-Semitic tack dictated by nature.[48] In amplifying on this feature he carefully differentiated between the anti-Semitism of the intellec-

---

[47] Ştefănescu. *Filosofia Românească*, 182, 184, & 187.
[48] A. D. Xenopol, "Naţionalism şi Antisemitism" *Noua Revistă Română*, 5 (1909), nr. 18: 276; A. D. Xenopol, *Istoria partidelor politice în România* (Bucureşti: Albert Baer, 1910), 518.

tuals and that of the general population. His perception contended that the average Romanian vehemently opposed any and all concessions to the Jews in the area of equal rights, and he cited the mass demonstrations and petitions to back up this premise. The intelligentsia and political leadership shared the peasantry's emotional repugnance towards the Jewish community, but, due to embarrassment, they also exhibited a willingness to proceed in the direction of tolerance. Under pressure they felt obliged because of humanitarian considerations and the political prescripts of European civilization to circumscribe their instinctive anti-Semitism. Fortunately, from their and Xenopol's point of view the mass opposition to allowances for Jewish rights furnished a rationale for noncompliance. His list of priorities, then, placed devotion to country and culture second only to the preservation of one's own life. Or as he put it tailoring the philosophical dictum to his nationalistic purposes, after the first necessity of maintaining life we must love our fatherland ("Primum vivere deinde patriam amare" in place of "Primum vivere, deinde philosophari").[49]

Although Xenopol like others among the intelligentsia occasionally slipped into the use of derogatory terminology that summed up the whole battery of traditional accusations against the Jews (e.g. "Yid"), his anti-Semitism was less catholic. In fact he claimed that he did not qualify as an anti-Semite in the more mundane sense for he did not reject them for religious reasons but rather economic and cultural ones. He likewise thought that those who attempted to throw the cloak of religious intolerance over Romanian anti-Semitism had not only misunderstood its nature, but also committed a calumny against the Romanian nation.[50] On the contrary, the Jew for him was ultimately a foreigner who refused to speak Romanian, not a religious enemy. Instead of participating in the native culture of the Principalities this immigrant from Galicia or Russia persisted in expressing himself through what Xenopol described as "the intolerable jargon of Jewish-German" (i.e., Yiddish). If and when a Jew did attempt to use Romanian, Xenopol con-

---

[49] Xenopol, *Istoria partidelor politice*, 517–8; A. D. Xenopol, "Naționalismul," *Noua Revistă Română*, 5 (1908), nr. 3: 37.

[50] I. E. Torouțiu, *Studii și Documente Literare*, IV (București: Institutul de Arte Grafice "Bucovina," 1933), 416–7; Xenopol, *Istoria partidelor politice*, 512.

tended that he so mutilated the language as to antagonize those who heard him. As an inveterate foreigner refusing to employ the vernacular, the Jew also became in Xenopol's eyes a member of a transnational establishment intruding in the nation's life. This jargon-spouting individual shared neither the language nor the mentality of the Romanian people. Xenopol in addition attacked the country's Jewish community for an alleged patronizing attitude towards Romanian culture that singled them out among the world's Jewish populations. His hurt pride showed in that he complained that French, Italian, and Spanish Jews all learned and spoke their host countries' languages. But Jews in Romania, even when they were third generation residents, still misused the mother tongue. When the discussions over Jewish naturalization began, Xenopol was adamant that the major criterion for the granting of citizenship had to be a perfect knowledge of the Romanian language. This command of the vernacular would, of course, likewise indicate that the Jews of the country had passed the test of embracing Romanian traditions and aspirations.[51]

Xenopol's xenophobia took on an especially interesting cast when he dealt with the subject of assimilation; namely, intermarriage between Romanian gentiles and the Jewish community. To begin with he experienced political attacks accusing him of being at least part Jewish. His defense consisted in claiming an Anglo-Saxon, Protestant background as well as an original family name of Brunswick. The logic and consistency of Romanian anti-Semitism also surfaced in his claim that his father could not have been Jewish, since he had been baptized. Given his own definition of nationality as being primarily cultural in foundation, this obviously constitutes a *non sequitur*. However much he claimed his anti-Semitism had no religious component, the factor of faith at least as a patina reappeared continuously.[52] The foundation of Xenopol's anti-Semitism rested on the view that the Jews in Romania composed a foreign nation. Given both their numbers (he gave five percent of the population as his figure) and their alien character, they would remain "a threat to the nation" until they

---

[51] A. D. Xenopol, "Patriotizmul," *Arhiva Societății științifice și literare din Iași*, XVII (1906), nr. 7/8: 347; Xenopol, "Naționalism și Antisemitism," 276-7.

[52] Toroutiu, *Studii și Documente Literare*, IV, 369 & 400.

assimilated. Here we should be careful to distinguish his notion of assimilation from more generous ones. He spoke not of simple acculturation but of the disappearance of the Jews as a recognizable community. In contrast to more radical, twentieth century anti-Semites Xenopol advocated intermarriage as the most powerful and sure means of absorbing this large, "alien," and potentially "menacing" group. As a prerequisite to marriage he specified that the Jews would have to be baptized. He saw this, however, not as a religious act or intolerance but rather as a means of removing impediments to the joining of different peoples. Whether or not he expected any sincerity or appreciated what a religious individual might identify as purity of intention cannot be determined. His reasoning was tortured at best. Xenopol maintained throughout his writings that this insistence on baptism rested on the secular conviction that only in this fashion could the Jewish race be incorporated into the Romanian. Since the Jews were a people without a country or a fatherland, this type of incisive but "nonreligious" action had to be carried out in order to protect Romanian traditions and values. He purportedly wished not to turn them into titular Christians, but to overcome what he saw as an inveterate adhesion to their sense of exclusivity. Xenopol stressed what he deemed this "particular race's" lack of a sense of a community of language and of nationality.[53]

If such an assimilation through intermarriage could be accomplished, Xenopol thought that Romania would gain in more than a politically nationalistic sense. Persisting in presenting himself as not being an anti-Semite, he claimed that "the introduction of Jewish blood" would bring to the Romanian race valuable qualities not currently to be found among its members. A disguised or submerged Jewish component in the country's makeup would give it an economic ability, a taste and talent for the marketplace, which it lacked.[54] In asserting that the Jew should intermarry and had a significant contribution to make to the Romanian stock line, Xenopol certainly set himself apart from the fanatic fringe of anti-Semites. He did not, however, think this fusion likely. Unfortunately his perception persisted that a Jew "was a Jew" before anything

---

[53] Xenopol, "Naționalism și Antisemitism," 277; Xenopol, "Patriotizmul," 348–9.
[54] Torouțiu, *Studii și Documente Literare,* IV, 416–7.

else; namely, this ethno-religious awareness took precedence over nationalistic factors as well as over those of the intellect and judgment. He especially objected to what he highlighted as the Jewish tendency to place their group loyalty before more sublime conditions such as being a philosopher or a man of science. Compounding the threats of excessive immigration and disparity of language then, the Jewish community in Romania stood apart from the norm of the family of nations by obstinately refusing to assimilate. Apparently, Xenopol saw nothing contradictory in assailing his country's Jews for being Jewish first and foremost, while himself maintaining that being singularly if not parochially Romanian merited praise.[55]

Mildly critical of the politicians who in the independence crisis compromised their anti-Semitism to obtain Western recognition, Xenopol adhered adamantly to the xenophobic element in his nationalism. For him no choice existed except to emancipate Romania from the foreign influence of the Jews. The Jewish community had to be removed or at least diminished, but not *per se* because they were Jews. Like any other foreign contingent resident in the country and unwilling to assimilate or achieve some level of proficiency in the native language, they had this coming. Once again on this crucial point Xenopol leaves us wondering exactly what might be entailed in a "diminished" Jewish presence. On the one hand he categorically rejected hate or brutality, favoring instead economic means of confining their impact on the nation. He emphasized encouraging and training Romanians to take their places in the economy though recognizing the lack of suitable native capacity in most instances. He contended the goal of his nationalism and anti-Semitism was not violence but rather only the subjugation of the intruding ethnic group. On the other hand he called for a "war against foreign elements" in which the invading factor was not simply to be combatted but eliminated, if it endangered the Romanian core of the nation. The unique component of Xenopol's, and ultimately of Romania's, anti-Semitism resided in the deliberate embracing of a policy of restricted bias against the Jewish community. He called for war but one with definite "limits." While acknowledging

---

[55] Ibid., 417; A. D. Xenopol, "Opul lui Edgar Quinet 'La création'," *Convorbiri literare*, 4 (1870), nr. 14: 230.

the difficulty of deciding where and how to restrain this inherent Romanian anti-Semitism, Xenopol excluded the exaggerated nationalism of the chauvinist from his schematic of an acceptable prejudice. As minor and grudging as this boundary on violence and hatred may be, his *"rational* nationalism" (*sic*) did impress an important, variant character upon Romania's anti-Jewish partiality. Should they prove useful to the nation, then, they might be incorporated into it or left relatively undisturbed in what he defined as their otherwise objectionable pattern of ethnic behavior. But even if they constituted a danger, there could not be "a war of annihilation" directed against them. In this context Xenopol developed the intelligentsia's sense of accommodation with widespread discrimination, but ruled out a more ruthless vendetta requiring the total physical purging of the Jewish people. In twentieth century terms, he helped create a mentality that could allow for savage, quite extended pogroms but which balked at genocide. Xenopol called for a nationalism, and hence for an anti-Semitism, that would be "moderate and sagacious, one that would be useful in strengthening the Romanian people"—not an especially elevated attitude but one that would contribute to a monumental difference in the fate of hundreds of thousands of members of the Romanian Jewish community.[56]

Nicolae Iorga (1871–1940) represented the bridge and commanding influence between the generation of Romania's independence and that of World War II. As described by the country's equivalent of an intellectual elite's *Who's Who*, he possessed the most extraordinary mind ever given to the nation. As a leading player in the post-1881 intelligentsia he exercised enormous sway in developing, preserving, and purifying Romania's historical heritage.[57] Among Iorga's amazing list of accomplishments we find his nomination to the Romanian Academy while still in his twenties, corresponding membership in numerous foreign national academies, the rectorship of the University of Bucharest, an active political life that included election to Parliament and the post of prime minister,

---

[56] Torouțiu, *Studii și Documente Literare,* IV, 390; Xenopol, "Naționalism și Anti-semitism," 276–8.

[57] Lucian Predescu, *Enciclopedia cugetarea* (București: Georgescu Delafras, 1940), 437; Kanner, *La Société,* 236.

FIGURE VIII. Nicolae Iorga. From: *Nicolae Iorga* by B. Theodorescu. *Editura Științifică și Enciclopedică.*

a host of journalistic efforts, and a personal bibliography that runs to hundreds of items. That such a towering cultural and political figure also espoused anti-Semitism gave it a virtually irresistible panache. For him as for the other Romanian anti-Semites we have been analyzing, nationalism automatically encompassed a predominant anti-Jewish component. Indeed, he ended up "equating 'true' nationalism with anti-Semitism." The segment of the intelligentsia that reached positions of influence or governmental authority in the interwar period, then, felt not only his impact as a teacher/scholar, but also as the definitive spokesman for a peculiarly Romanian mode of anti-Semitism. In the course of over forty years' teaching, he shaped the cultural consciousness of thousands of students. In his writings, both scholarly and popular, he reached many more, contributing his authority to a form of nationalism that left little room for the hundreds of thousands of Jews living in Romania.[58] Ironically, among the individuals decisively influenced by Iorga's anti-Semitism was Corneliu Codreanu, the founder of the Romanian fascist organization the Iron Guard. Codreanu imbibed Iorga's identification of nationalism with anti-Semitism as well as his advocacy of a solution to "the Jewish Problem." Despite sharing a basic anti-Semitic posture with this group, Iorga criticized its impact on the Romanian government as well as expressed reservations regarding the hegemony in Europe of Hitler's Germany. For these foibles the preeminent champion of traditional Romanian anti-Semitism was assassinated in the fall of 1940 by the Iron Guard's Legionary Police. The new totalitarian, implacable anti-Semitism had no room for the conditional prejudice of Romania's outstanding twentieth century intellectual.[59]

In prescribing the primal tenor and thrust of Romania's anti-Semitism in this century, Iorga portrayed the Jew as "a commercial parasite and a vampire." Although rejecting the Jews as fellow citizens and comrades in the process of building the nation, Iorga did not descend to the level of employing ethnic epithets as we have seen others doing. This may have been a matter of style and class, however, since he did not hesitate to blame the massive jacquerie of 1907 on the Jewish community. Although himself a Moldavian and fully aware of the complex of causes of that province's poverty, Iorga identified the Jews with the horrific conditions experienced by the peasantry.[60] In his determined pursuit of a common and homogeneous national culture, he likewise accepted the notion of

[58] Bela Vago, *The Shadow of the Swastika, The Rise of Fascism and Anti-Semitism in the Danube Basin, 1936–1939* (London: Institute for Jewish Affairs, 1975), 56; Şt. Zeletin, *Burghezia română* (Bucureşti: Cultura Naţională, 1925), 228.

[59] Armon, "'Enemies' and 'Traitors'," 67–8; William O. Oldson, *The Historical and Nationalistic Thought of Nicolae Iorga* (Boulder & New York: East European Monographs, Columbia University Press, 1973), 9–10.

[60] N. Iorga, "In Chestia Evreiasca, De Ce Emigrează Evreii?, I," *Epoca*, 8 (1902), nr. 2034–213: 1; N. Iorga, "Răscoale ţerăneşti," *Neamul Românesc*, 1 (1907), nr. 86: 522.

the Jews as "agents of Germanization." Thus such a community seemed to him to be an affront to the nation's birthright of exclusive possession of the patrimonial territory. Believing as he did in the "divine right of existence" of the Romanian people and that "moral necessity" dictated their sole enjoyment of the country's bounty, in his more extreme utterance, Iorga called for the disappearance of all foreigners from Romanian soil.[61]

The core of his nationalism and perhaps the slogan best summing up his anti-Semitic orientation Iorga offered us in the context of the peasant revolt in the first decade of the twentieth century: "Romania for the Romanians, for all the Romanians, and only for the Romanians." Within this purview he defined the Jew as both an exploiter and as someone who profited by the sufferings of the Romanians.[62] In rounding out his formulation of anti-Semitism, though, Iorga insisted upon a positive element. The true Romanian patriot, according to his lights, should love his country for it was, not for what economic opportunities it might afford him. Having framed this prescription as a reproach to the Jewish community as much as a goal for the native Romanians, Iorga further developed the concept of a moral imperative by contending that the staunch nationalist had an obligation to love his people. In addition he asserted that the only "healthy races" were those who displayed profoundly nationalistic and patriotic sentiments. The Jewish community failed Iorga's test for Romanian nationalism on two counts; first because of what he termed exploitative activities and second they exhibited no deep attachment to the Romanian cultural and historical heritage. Instead they flaunted distinct signs of having their own national agenda and characteristics. His xenophobia could not tolerate this foreign element within the country and the possible alteration of its socio-economic base.[63]

[61] N. Iorga, *Correspondance diplomatique roumaine sous le roi Charles Ier (1866–1880)*. Deuxième édition (Bucarest: Bibliothèque de l'Institut pour l'Étude de l'Histoire Universelle, 1938), 269; N. Iorga, "In Chestia Evreiasca, III Doctrina de apărare economică," *Epoca*, 8 (1902), nr. 2077–175: 1; N. Iorga, "Sentiment național și ideie națională," *Neamui Romănesc*, 4 (1909), nr. 147–8: 2495.

[62] "Romănia a Romînilor, a tuturor Romînilor, numai a Romînilor," in N. Iorga, "Romîni și străini," *Neamul Romănesc*, 1 (1907), nr. 93: 629.

[63] N. Iorga, "Sîntem noi șoviniști?," *Neamul Romănesc*, 1 (1906), nr. 66: 194; N. Iorga, Speech to Adunarea Deputaților in *Desbaterile Adunării Deputaților*, nr. 45 (February 13, 1910): 597.

As with virtually every other influential anti-Semite we have
discussed, Iorga, too, contended that hatred of the Jews *per
se* does not exist among the Romanians and has no place in
their nationalism. The sentiments we have seen were expressed
during the negotiations for Romanian independence; namely,
that the matter at issue was national survival, not primarily
the Jews, and that Romanians had never embraced such
medieval attitudes as hating this minority for religious reasons.[64] Rather he preached that nationalism manifested itself
as a "natural" emotional and intellectual expression of humanity,
one motivated by a loving desire to protect one's people and
not by any inherent proclivity towards violence. He carefully
distinguished, at least to his own satisfaction, between the joyful
nationalism he endorsed and what he depicted as the coldly
cerebral arrogance of the chauvinist. Iorga's nationalist sought
to protect and preserve his heritage and an exclusive control
over traditional Romanian territories. His chauvinist acknowledged no other nation as having precedence over his own in
any regard. The chauvinist's nation represented the best in
the world. In attempting to establish this distinction Iorga
wanted to prove that he and his followers were indeed nationalists and democrats above all else, not anti-Semites. Thus,
for him there existed not a Jewish question, but a "Jewish
danger." He did not attack the Jewish community for its essential qualities differentiating it from the Romanian, but because
of its alleged exploitation of the nation's economy.[65] Defined
in this fashion, anti-Semitism became for him a permanent
issue, one transcending governments with their ephemeral
interests. Seeking to avoid the pejorative connotations of this
prejudice Iorga stressed his view that this aspect of Romanian
nationalism was a "positive" one treating the ethnic and historical rights of the people. He claimed to abhor the violence,
both verbal and physical, to be found in more extremist versions of anti-Semitism. He simply wished in a xenophobic
manner to exclude foreign meddling in Romanian affairs as
well as any evidence of a distinct and separate Jewish public.

---

[64] N. Iorga, "In Chestia Evreiasca, IV Tipurile evreești: proletarul," *Epoca*, 8 (1902),
nr. 2087–185: 1; N. Iorga, *Politica externa a Regelui Carol I* (București: Institutul de Arte
Grafice Luceafarul S. A., 1923), 319.

[65] Iorga, "Sîntem noi șoviniști?," 194; N. Iorga, "În chestia evreiască," *Neamul
Românesc*, 4 (1909), nr. 88: 1401–2.

In the end, therefore, Iorga called for a purportedly humane anti-Semitism. Since the faults and lack of certain economic traits on the part of the Romanians had given the Jews their chance in the country, the solution to this problem lay not in persecution or hatred. Iorga saw these manifestations of anti-Semitism as childish and barbarous. In their place he called for the development of Romanian society to the extent that the Jews would no longer be necessary and would simply depart. He would not mercilessly hunt down and exterminate the Jewish community as intrinsically abhorrent. He just did not want them in his nation.[66]

These men, and the lesser ones following their lead, resuscitated traditional patterns of culture. They and their writings helped form the Romanian intelligentsia in all its lineaments, including anti-Semitism. They played active roles in the educational process that turned out intellectuals who exhibited the bravado of nationalistic mavens. The shop owners, bureaucrats, professional men, proprietors of estates all read the works of this anti-Semitic elite incorporating its message into their own views. The peasant population, the vast majority of Romanians, expressed its anti-Semitism crudely and as in the uprising of 1907 with extraordinary violence. But the educated few used their access to political power to manipulate the state. They could now implement the theories of culture this intellectual patriciate had created for them. Though the raw materials of anti-Semitism had long been present, the intelligentsia fashioned a distinguished model for Romanian nationalistic culture. Such an ethnic exemplar left no place for an unassimilated Jewish community. This group of six seminal thinkers on the topic of anti-Semitism possessed what has aptly been termed "the political missionary drive." Either through active participation in the political arena or in tracts designed to influence educated public opinion they directed the state into an anti-Semitic channel. By similar strategies they bred subsequent generations of anti-Jewish intellectuals. Their influence has been a lasting one, imparting characteristics to Romanian anti-Semitic bias that remain until the present. In short, they created and spoke for a strain of Romanian thought that broadly influenced governmental actions as well as popular sentiments

---

[66] Iorga, Speech to the Adunarea Deputaților, 591–3.

on minority issues throughout the last half of the nineteenth century and all of the present one. Even in the rise of a native fascist movement in the 1930s and in the actions of the dictatorship of World War II the profound impact of these men was still to be seen.[67]

In assessing the impact of these highly visible and influential anti-Semites we must appreciate the fact that they represented more than a virulent form of nationalism. They also symbolized the nation's rejection of the allegedly "cosmopolitan" influences often associated with the Jewish poulation. This xenophobia was endemic in the other Balkan countries as well at the turn of the century. But on the Romanian scene it equated an extraordinary emphasis on national values with a profound anti-Semitism. In fact for many this bias became the cardinal attribute of their nationalism. It led to a peculiarly Romanian discussion on the qualitative differences between various Jewish communities as well as on the relationship between constitutional rights and the perceived caliber of a human being. As we will see in the next chapter, the spokesmen for Romanian nationalism demonstrated a marvelously adept ability to employ successfully this mental construct to further the aims of their anti-Semitism.[68]

---

[67] Elena Siupiur, "The Training of Intellectuals in South-East Europe during the 19th Century. The Romanian Model," *Anuarul Institutul de Istorie și Arheologie "A. D. Xenopol,"* 23 (1986): 469–72 & 477; John H. Jensen & Gerhard Rosegger, "Xenophobia or Nationalism? The Demands of the Romanian Engineering Profession for Preference in Government Contracts, 1898–1905," *East European Quarterly*, 19 (1985), nr. 1: 1.

[68] Kanner, *La Société*, 62–3; Jensen, "Xenophobia or Nationalism," 11; Zeletin, *Burghezia română*, 230.

The Quality of Our Jews

The political maneuvering as well as the theorizing associated with the Jewish question in Romania did not take place in a vacuum. The purpose of all that we have seen thus far remained constant; namely, to prevent any appreciable introduction of naturalized Jewish citizens into the life of the Romanian nation. Nowhere can we find a more penetrating insight into this mentality and into the consequences for the minority under attack than in the discussion of "quality." Romanian politicians and the ideologues of the intelligentsia developed a schema according to which they differentiated gentile from Jew on the basis of perceived, inherent worth. They furthermore elaborated and managed to convince a significant number of influential individuals outside of Romania, both gentile and Jewish, that material distinctions existed between various types of Jews. This might well have been expected. The success of the anti-Semite and the moment that success had for the question of Jewish rights in the country lay, however, in the peculiar leap of logic that then linked the constitutional rights of citizenship with these purported differences in quality. This concept of "Jewish quality" allowed the anti-Semite not only the luxury of indulging his bias with some considerable flourish, but also to take a more reasonable and defensible stand when confronting the criticisms of the foreigner. Having persuaded the outside observer of the disparate levels of Jewish culture, the Romanian nationalist did not have to concede the moral high ground. He could rationalize the continued lack of progress towards Jewish naturalization in a style less impeachable by the rest of Europe. The ideology of quality, therefore, tendered the Romanian anti-Semite the intellectual weapon to disarm some of the criticism from abroad. Likewise he could justify in his own mind the failure to fulfill the strictures of the revised Article 7 of the nation's constitution. In short, the argument based on quality masked the insincerity of Romania's effort to carry out the clearly understood intent of Article XLIV of the Congress of Berlin. It certainly foreshadowed the dismal record of Jewish access to citizenship up to the time of World War I.

This approach to the "Jewish Question" as well as the practicalities of rendering Europe more benevolent towards Romanian independence surfaced in the naturalizations just prior to the granting of diplomatic recognition. In this instance the government agreed to the en masse bestowal of citizenship on approximately one thousand Jews. As we have seen most of these were veterans. Just as importantly, they enjoyed the correct socioeconomic credentials. One approach to the matter of Jewish quality found its expression in defining only the rich and educated as possessing the appropriate quality to merit equality of rights. Assimilation based on these criteria of wealth and a veneer of Western culture would automatically exclude most of the Jews in Romania from any chance of eventually becoming citizens.[1] The confining animus of the government displayed itself by mid-1879 in the list of specifications discussed with the Germans regarding the types of Jews which might someday receive citizenship papers. Clearly, the Romanian government wanted to circumscribe both the numbers and the circumstances of these involved. The individual exhibiting the demeanor of the Galician or Russian Jewish heritage fell outside the horizon envisaged as permissible. The entire non-Sephardic community, then, could not qualify under these idiosyncratic standards. Either for reasons of Hasidic eccentricity (i.e., costume and the use of Yiddish) or because they dealt with lower class concerns, the overwhelming majority of Jewish immigrants in Moldavia could never hope to meet Romanian expectations for the prospective citizen. Obviously, they would

---

[1] Joseph Berkowitz, *La Question des Israélites en Roumanie* (Paris: Jouve et Cie, 1923), 651; Petre Bărbulescu (ed.), *Reprezentanţele diplomatice ale României*, I (Bucureşti: Editura Politică, 1967), 48.

not become peasants, nor were they likely to embrace Romanian cultural traditions or achieve the ennoblement status of the bureaucrat. They must remain outside the pale due to their ethnic origins, the meanness of their pursuits, and the bizarreness of their culture. They lacked the quality, the breeding or refinement, as far as the Romanians assayed them to aspire to naturalization.[2]

The Romanian regard for the Jewish immigrant or resident alien in the period before the First World War began, then, with a certain stigmatization. This individual had infiltrated into the nation's territory and heritage in an unwelcome, if not always illegal, fashion. The numbers he represented (i.e., several hundreds of thousands) could not conceivably be integrated into the country's life without severe disruption of its nationalistic essentials. More disturbing yet in the Romanian politician's and nationalist's estimation this process of infiltration had not remained constant but accelerated by the midnineteenth century. This Hasidic *hoi polloi* threatened to disinherit the Romanian majority in areas identified with their national birthright,[3] so the Romanian government commenced very early to diagnose the acceptability of the "Spanish" Jew, while rejecting the "Polish" variety. The qualitative differences present in the Romanian perception decided both the question of equal rights and the nature of the bureaucratic harassment that would accompany any attempt to secure naturalization. The Galician-Russian community offered only a religiously oriented, uncouth type of Jew whom the Romanian nationalist could not conceive of as a useful citizen.[4]

Having arrived at this working concept of "quality" as a means of circumventing unwelcome but unavoidable foreign intervention in their domestic affairs, the Romanian anti-Semites had to convince the outsider of his ignorance of the

---

[2] *Aus dem Leben König Karls von Rumänien; Aufzeichnungen eines Augenzeugen*, IV (Stuttgart: Cotta'sche Buchhandlung, 1900), 232; Frédéric Damé, *Histoire de la Roumanie Contemporaine* (Paris: Germer Baillière et Cie, 1900), 315–6.

[3] Mihail Kogălniceanu, *Opere*, V. Georgeta Penelea (ed.), (București: Editura Academiei Republicii Socialiste România, 1984), 9.

[4] Martin Winckler, "Bismarcks Rumänienpolitik und die Durchführung des Artikels 44 des Berliner Vertrages (1878–1880)." Ph.D. Dissertation, Ludwig-Maximilians-Universität zu München, 1951, 128; Nicholas M. Nagy-Talavera, *The Green Shirts and the Others, A History of Fascism in Hungary and Rumania* (Stanford: Hoover Institution Press, 1970), 44.

local scene. Furthermore, this observer had to be enticed to see the nefarious influence of the Western Jewish press, particularly where "precise information" on conditions in Romania was involved. As indicated in contemporary diplomatic correspondence, the Foreign Minister in Bucharest and the Romanian agent in Rome subscribed to and attempted to exploit the stereotypical caricature of "the unfavorable influence of Jewish coteries," especially in the Italian press. And qualitative discrepancies between types of Jews constituted a paramount segment of this "precise information" the nationalist wished to convey and that these "Jewish coteries" would attempt to dispute.[5] The earliest endorsement of the Romanian view of Jewish quality came from the Russian Empire in the person of Prince Gorchakov during his participation at the Congress of Berlin. This aristocratic statesman divided "Eastern and Western Jews" qualitatively and territorially by a line of demarcation extending along the Austro-Hungarian Empire's easternmost frontier. Whatever the Jews of Western Europe might be like, those beyond the Habsburg march endured as a deliberately extraneous factor in Romanian national existence. As the Romanians proclaimed repeatedly not only during the struggle for diplomatic recognition but throughout the nineteenth century, so too Gorchakov maintained that in Russia the Jewish question had never involved the principle of religious liberty. This humanitarian doctrine he asserted had always been conceded by the Russian government and given the most generous of applications. But like the Romanians he drew the line at civil and political rights. In severing religious rights from those of citizenship, Gorchakov based his case on the ostensible qualitative variations between "the Jews of Berlin, Paris, London, or Vienna . . . [and those] of Romania and some Russian provinces. . . ." To the first group he would not deny any of the civil or political prerogatives normally associated with citizenship. The second category he and the Romanians viewed as a scourge and a calamity for the areas in which they lived. Anticipating the specious line of reasoning to be utilized by the Romanians, Gorchakov argued that significant cultural dissimilarities existed between gentile and Jew in Eastern Europe,

---

[5] Raoul V. Bossy, *Politica externă a României între anii 1873–1880 privită dela Agenția diplomatică din Roma* (București: Cultura Națională, 1928), 15–6.

as well as between the communities of Jews throughout the continent. Therefore, while religious liberty had to be extended to the Jewish minority, incorporation into the body politic was unwise, unnecessary, and not mandated by the grand principles of civilization then being bandied about. Quite obviously the prince comported himself in this instance primarily as a spokesman for Russian interests and the Empire's image in Western Europe. Though sympathetic to the Romanian predicament, he did not intend to make a determined stand in their behalf and certainly did not care to expend any political capital for a wartime ally so casually manipulated during the Congress.[6]

During the sessions of the Congress the Romanians never made this argument. When Kogălniceanu and Brătianu delivered their speeches, they concentrated on trying to prevent the loss of territory linked with Romanian claims for independence, especially that of Bessarabia. Neither advocate of the nationalistic cause even mentioned the issue of Jewish rights during the session of 1 July to which they were admitted grudgingly by the Great Powers. In the course of the debate that followed, the thesis grounded on the qualitative issue swayed no one's vote. Waddington, the French Foreign Minister and champion of the altruistic faction, acknowledged that "local difficulties" might exist in Romania but still carried the day for the insertion of Article XLIV into the Congress's deliberations. He optimistically contended that once Romania granted its Jews freedom of religion and equality of rights these provincial obstacles would more easily be overcome. Romanian Jewry could then by its own efforts eventually arrive at a position of common interest, if not solidarity, with the autochthonous population. In the end all participants accepted the French line. Russia supported France without withdrawing her self-serving position relative to Jewish quality, choosing to concentrate on obtaining Bessarabia.[7]

The naïve French stance on possible Romanian-Jewish accom-

[6] Nagy-Talavera, *The Green Shirts and the Others*, 48; "Protocole No. 8. Séance du 28 Juin 1878," *Nouveau recueil général de Traités, et autres actes relatifs aux rapports de droit international*. Continuation du grant recueil de G. Fr. de Martens, III (Göttingen: Librairie de Dieterich, 1878), 341–2.

[7] "Protocole No. 10. Séance du 1er Juillet 1878, *Nouveau recueil général de Traités*, 358–70.

modation and the concession that "local difficulties" might exist
provided the anti-Semite as well as the government with a
more respectable means of resisting the exigencies of Article
XLIV. Paris rescued them from simply having to be blatantly
anti-Jewish in the usual trite manner. Rather than a crude reversion to timeworn anti-Semitic stereotypes (though this too
occurred), the nationalist could make his case at least in part
by playing upon his listeners' own reactions to the Hasidim.
Although the Congress had persisted in requiring some adaptation by Romania in the realm of religious liberties, the door
had been opened to the interpretation and manipulation of
this euphemism. Enough sentiment gradually developed to
allow the Romanian anti-Semite to expatiate upon the theme
of quality to delay and frustrate the mandated naturalization
process. From the very beginning of the diplomatic effort to
obtain full diplomatic recognition of the country's independence, then, Romania's representatives abroad harped on the
variations in quality and character between their Jews and those
found elsewhere. They pursued this motif in an especially assid-
uous fashion due to the numbers involved. Reading their correspondence there can be no doubt that the presence of hundreds of thousands of "Polish Jews" brought the quality
contention to the fore. It likewise permitted the fabrication of
a gentler facade, one less provoking to some elements of West
European opinion.[8]

Mihai Eminescu expressed most eloquently the typical Romanian argument relating to the quality of the Jews resident in
the Principalities. His starting point focused on extremely few
of the Jews in Romania possessing any attributes which would
make them "useful" to the state or national interest. Those
few who merited citizenship invariably did so because they
possessed the individual characteristics and worth of the
"Spanish Jews."[9] Eminescu's adamantly held opinion posited
that without the "personal value" associated with the West-
ernized culture of the nonHasidic Jews, there could be no ques-

---

[8] Bossy, *Politica externă a României,* 190.

[9] By "Spanish Jews" Eminescu and the other Romanian anti-Semites meant the
traditional Sephardic community which sought refuge in the Ottoman Empire after
its expulsion from the Iberian peninsula. Associated with a considerable higher level
of learning and social status, this group spoke Ladino or Judeo-Spanish rather than
the Yiddish of the Hasidim so much despised by Romanian nationalists.

tion of apportioning the benefits postulated in the Congress's protocols. Once this exceptional group received equality of rights, he believed the requirements of Article XLIV as well as the prescriptions of a humane civilization had been satisfied. In qualitative terms the "Spanish" and "Polish" Jews had nothing in common.[10] In a provocative twist to this aspect of Danubian anti-Semitism, Bogdan Petriceicu Hasdeu professed that all Romanians not merely saw a difference in quality between "foreign" Jews and "our own," but admired the occasional cultured Romanian Jew. A self-consciously proclaimed esteem for a minuscule elite, then, went hand in hand with the utmost contempt and condescension for the bulk of Romanian Jewry. The tone of this argument, one that continued beyond the period under study well into the twentieth century in the writings of others like Nicolae Iorga, echoed the refrain that all these anti-Semites had many Jewish friends. But they were always of the right sort and an exception from the usual level of the Jewish community. Apparently this superior Jew also did not resent the anti-Semitic rhetoric expressed by these men or the patronizing attitude.[11] A final strand of the thesis acording to quality was the view that the lesser type of Jew also contaminated the Latin characteristics of the nation. In fact the Hasidim "germanized" their environment and all that came into contact with it. The indigenous Jewish community, through its foreignness and ignoble mien, constantly proved that it did not merit the concession of citizenship. Its inferior quality resided in the ethnic birthmark it bore as well as in the stratum of culture to which it belonged. Utterly convinced of the qualitative discrepancy between native and foreign Jews, the Romanian anti-Semites proceeded with the task of gaining at least marginal acceptance abroad for this view. More importantly they had to establish a binding connection between a community of inferior quality and the possibility of denying that group full equality of rights.[12]

---

[10] M. Eminescu, *Opera politică*, I(1870–1879), I. Crețu (ed.), (București: Cugetarea—Georgescu Delafras, 1941), 97–8, 102, 108, & 498; D. Murărașu, *Naționalismul lui Eminescu* (București: Institutul de Arte Grafice "Bucovina" I. E. Torouțiu, 1932), 146.

[11] Bogdan Petriceicu Hasdeu, *Scrieri Literare, Morale și Politice*, II. Mircea Eliade (ed.), (București: Fundația pentru Literatură și Artă "Regele Carol II," 1937), 333–4.

[12] N. Iorga, *Correspondence diplomatique roumaine sous le roi Charles Ier (1866–1880)*. Deuxième édition (Bucarest: Bibliothèque de l'Institut pour l'étude de l'Histoire Universelle, 1938), 269; Kogălniceanu, *Opera*, V, 9.

This conceit regarding variations in quality between types of Jews never achieved widespread official acceptance outside of Romania and Russia. However Romanian anti-Semites did encounter enough positive, or at least not vehemently opposed, reactions to encourage the use of this tactic. The fact that anyone in an influential position would placidly listen to this argument, and then perhaps countenance it, gave the new Kingdom of Romania the eagerly sought opportunity for evasion of significant numbers of Jewish naturalizations. The sympathy and understanding expressed by some foreigners likewise breached any Western common front for criticizing Romanian lack of action in the area of equality of rights. Now there arose Western voices which favored Jewish rights, but counseled restraint due to the inarguable chasm in quality between Western and Eastern Jewry. Having endorsed the humanitarian principles contained in Article XLIV of the Congress of Berlin, the country could not seriously be expected to enfranchise hundreds of thousands of recently arrived "Polish" Jews. The fascinating even if puzzling mental processes which allowed outsiders to criticize legalized intolerance in Romania, but then acquiesce in a qualitatively dictated double standard appeared most strikingly in the case of Italy. From the very beginning of Romanian efforts to obtain independence and diplomatic recognition the Italian foreign office had advised Bucharest that its refusal to grant equality comprised both a political mistake and an unconscionable contravention of European standards for humane government. Rome further insisted that it would allow no distinctions between its gentile and Jewish citizens on the part of the Romanians. But having specified these points, the Italian bureaucracy went on to sanction the Romanian thesis of the characteristically different quality of Eastern Jews. Since these Jews brought with them a "germanizing" influence detrimental to the Latin nature of the nation, Rome signified its willingness to see restrictions imposed on them on a nonreligious basis.[13]

Cultural disabilities elicited assent if not enthusiasm, once the pro forma ritual of acknowledging sectarian freedom had been performed. Perhaps the Italians did not comprehend the

---

[13] *Documente privind istoria României, Războiul pentru independență,* III (București: Editura Academiei Republicii Populare Române, 1953), 422–3.

intensity of the Romanians' aversion or the adroitness they would demonstrate in implementing the doctrine of differences in quality, for by this time the cultural assimilation of Italian Jews was such that "the profession of Judaism was regarded as an amiable eccentricity rather than a social mistake." Unfortunately, in Romania Jewishness transcended a mere miscue and certainly did not appear to the anti-Semite as a fetching nonconformity. It rendered the individual redundant and undesirable in a highly charged nationalist milieu. The Romanian appreciation of foreign comprehension on this point as well as the import they attached to it surfaced once again in their diplomatic agent's report in January of 1880. At this point near the terminus of the recognition contest, the foreign minister in Bucharest was informed of a "very cordial" conversation with the Italian king. In the course of this dialogue King Humbert I described how he had been instructed about the nature of Romanian Jews by one of the leading anti-Semites of the day. He went on to convey his admiration for this anti-Jewish intellectual and to acknowledge the difference between "our Jews [i.e., Romanian] and the Jews of Italy." Humbert also cautioned that this qualitative difference had not been fully accepted by the Italian parliament, especially its Jewish members. Therefore the Romanians should step up their efforts to make this point more convincingly.[14]

A quite explicit accreditation of this apologia according to quality was forthcoming from the British government. In the course of the summer of 1879 London had received two lengthy, detailed briefs from the Romanians stressing the character of their Jewish population.[15] The reasoning of the theses centered on the peculiar problems inherent in the Romanian Jewish question as a rationale for not meeting the expectations of the Western Powers. As had the Italians, Lord Salisbury both acknowledged the difficulties faced by Bucharest and deplored the treatment of Romanian Jews. But despite his government's publicly stated position on Article XLIV the British foreign minister deferred to the Romanian theme of qualitatively deficient

---

[14] Cecil Roth, *The History of the Jews of Italy* (Philadelphia: The Jewish Publication Society of America, 1946), 474–5; Bossy, *Politica externă a României*, 211–2.

[15] "Correspondence relative to the Recognition of the Independence of Roumania – 1879–1880," *British and Foreign State Papers*, Vol. 71 (1879–1880). (London: William Ridgway, 1887), 1149–56 & 1158–62.

Jews. If the Romanians would accept the ideal of toleration,
then Salisbury agreed that "It might be necessary to exercise
caution in admitting at once to the rights of citizenship multi-
tudes who were not in a condition of education or civilization
which would enable them to exercise those rights to the advantage of the community."[16] Besides succumbing to Romanian
justifications on the issue of merit, Lord Salisbury also either
ignored or did not fathom that "caution" on the lower Danube
meant probably never. If these Jews persisted in their uniqueness, then they could not reach appropriate levels of education
or civilization from the Romanian point of view. In gauging
the recalcitrance of the Romanian government and the success
it enjoyed from 1878–1914 in denying naturalization to its Jewish
population, we must recognize that some Jews perceived their
Hasidic kin as inferior. Certainly the wealthier, traditional
Sephardic Jews of Bucharest did not care for the outside intrusion relative to the dictates of the Congress of Berlin. More
to the point, influential Western Jews like the Viennese Moritz
Ritter von Goldschmidt (an intimate of Bleichröder and involved
with the Rothschilds for decades) on occasion declared that
en bloc according of full equality to Romania's Jewish population should not be pursued.[17] This equivocal mentality sup-
portive of the Romanian position can best be epitomized in
Goldschmidt's own words: "[not] *everything* that the Rumanian
Jews hoped to achieve could be attained at one time; . . . considering that in Austria we have attained the present condition only gradually, and we are, God knows, better people
than our Rumanian coreligionists."[18] This muted though clear
sanction of the quality contention by Western gentile and Jew
alike afforded the Romanian government more than ample
scope for insincerity and avoiding the enfranchisement fore-
seen in the debates at Berlin.

From the very beginning of the contest over the status of
the Jews in Romania the interplay between public relations
and lack of basic good will evidenced itself. In July of 1878 Prince
Carol's father, Karl Anton, wrote giving him advice that in gen-

---

[16] Ibid., 1165–6.
[17] Fritz Stern, *Gold and Iron. Bismarck, Bleichröder, and the Building of the German Empire* (New York: Vintage Books, 1979), 57, 374, & 386.
[18] Ibid., 386.

eral terms influenced future Romanian actions. Karl Anton's appraisal pointed out that the equal rights provision of Article XLIV simply constituted a "humanitarian phrase." Once accepted the Western Great Powers would be eager to relegate administration of the edict to the normal legislative procedures or at worst to a special committee. In either case the new Kingdom of Romania could have its own way.[19] Foreign awareness of both the public relations gambit being pursued by Romania as well as that state's insincerity on the issue of Jewish rights received confirmation throughout the diplomatic process. By the summer of 1879 the Italian government was advising Bucharest of the necessity of a "quasi-commitment" to quiet domestic opposition and allow for the earliest possible deployment of an ambassador. The British and German governments each thought that the Romanians had built a facade behind which to hide their true intentions vis-à-vis their Jews. Lord Salisbury put it most aptly when he commented that the Romanian sense of obligation in this matter seemed to him ". . . to be merely an act of grace towards certain individuals, not the acceptance of a principle."[20] By the late summer of 1879 the Romanian government had clearly expressed its determination to execute the requirements of Article XLIV only "within the limits of the possible." And the quality of its Jews largely determined "the possible." Salisbury, having already acquiesced in the purported unsuitability of Eastern Jews for enfranchisement, translated this Romanian quasi-commitment into his own terms. Here the limits of the possible became what seemed "feasible" at the moment to the Romanians commissioned to carry out Berlin's mandate.[21]

With a clever bit of staging the Romanians planned, and then carried out, a strategy that involved the naturalization of a token number of assimilated Jews. While continuing to preclude any meaningful granting of equality of rights to the vast majority of Eastern Jews, they broadcast and had accepted to an amazing degree the doctrine of quality. Thus they presented themselves as not blatantly discriminating in the

---

[19] *Aus dem Leben*, 87.
[20] Bossy, *Politica externă*, 188–9; "Correspondence relative to the Recognition of the Independence of Roumania," 1157–8.
[21] "Correspondence relative to the Recognition," 1161–2 & 1165–6.

area of sectarian rights, but rather doing what they could given the destitute level of culture among the "Polish" Jews. One powerful element permitting the Great Powers to countenance this pretense as the only feasible one was the propaganda emphasizing the link between the prerogatives of citizenship and the quality of the human material involved.[22] That the Western Great Powers clearly understood the primacy of independence in the Romanian blueprint as well as the role that this lack of candor had in it there can be no doubt. With the Romanians supplying the tactical reason for doing so by emancipating a few acculturated Jews, the Great Powers could either look the other way or facilely explain their restraint by reference to the abysmal quality of the bulk of Romanian Jewry. The British indicated their willingness to look the other way, while the Germans demonstrated a remarkable forbearance of guile especially where their railroad investments were concerned.[23] A certain manifestation of this level of duplicity finally emerged in February of 1880 attendant upon the recognition of Romania as formally independent in the eyes of the Western Great Powers. The identical notes of recognition transmitted by France, Germany, and Great Britain all deplored the partial compliance of Romania with the strictures of the Congress of Berlin. But having saved face in this fashion, the three Powers then conceded the fundamental proposition that Romanian Jews had only the status of stateless persons (*"apatrid"*). What the Romanians surmised from the entire episode Prince Carol summed up in a letter to his father. Speaking of the Berlin treaty with its specifications relative to the Romanian Jewish problem and of the nature of the notes of recognition, he observed that in the fast paced nineteenth century all of this was already in the past. The patent implication that the Jews were old business could not be missed. Romania could and would do very much as she had done in the past relative to her Jewish inhabitants.[24]

---

[22] Titu Maiorescu, *Discursuri parlamentare*, (1876–1881), II (București: Editura Librăriei Socecǔ & Comp., 1897), 362 & 365; Winckler, "Bismarcks Rumänienpolitik," 175.

[23] *Documents diplomatiques français (1871–1914)*, 1re serie (1871–1900), V. 2 (Paris: Imprimerie Nationale, 1930), 401–2, 466–8, & 515–6; *Independența României, Documente, IV (Documente Diplomatice, 1873–1881)*, A. Gr. Paraipan, A. N. Popescu, & C. I. Turcu (eds.), (București: Editura Academiei Republicii Socialiste România, 1978), 433, 463–5, 524, 583, & 589.

[24] *Aus dem Leben*, 293–6.

In 1881, the definitive year of Romania's diplomatic triumph with the proclamation of the Kingdom, we also have the unambiguous statement of how she resolved the Jewish issue. C. A. Rosetti (1816–1885), one of the new nation's preeminent writers and politicians, announced that not only had Romania settled the question of Jewish rights in a nationalistic sense, but that it had been done ". . . contrary to the manifest will of the Powers and contrary even to the spirit of the Treaty of Berlin."[25] The Great Powers had set out to correct the legalized discrimination of the Romanian constitution and to promote Jewish enfranchisement to a degree not attainable under existing legislation. Most obviously this meant eradicating the prohibition against non–Christian naturalizations. They particularly wished to amend a situation allowing for not a single naturalized Jewish citizen between 1858 and 1866, even though such enfranchisement had been called for by the Paris conference of the latter year.[26] Unfortunately, in the newly proclaimed Kingdom of Romania, the legal status of the Jewish population deteriorated as a result of the compromise arrived at in the course of awarding diplomatic recognition to Bucharest. Despite a revised and superficially more humane constitution, Romanian Jews now became victims of a more encompassing nationalistic variety of anti-Semitism. Though the religious factor disappeared from Article 7, the Jews paid dearly for it in that they emerged from the diplomatic dickering defined officially as stateless. Between 1879 and 1914, then, the position of the Jewish population in Romania became more exacerbated, since the government's positions on citizenship and quality had both been conceded either formally or otherwise. And it soon became apparent that Romania's officialdom intended to enforce the procedures for naturalization in the most closefisted of fashions. But, through the Levantine construction put on the process, Romania could no longer be decried in the West as acting against its Jews. Rather Bucharest could simply claim that these foreigners had not met the criteria for the special act of the legislature required to dispense citizenship. This

---

[25] Carol Iancu, *Les Juifs en Roumanie (1866–1919), de l'Exclusion à l'Emancipation* (Aix-en-Provence: Editions de l'Université de Provence, 1978), 180.

[26] Ibid., 89; Berkowitz, *La Question des Israélites en Roumanie*, 285 & 292.

artifice worked as well as the Romanians hoped and the Jewish community feared.[27]

In the course of the parliamentary debates on revising Article 7 and accepting the toleration edict contained in Article XLIV of the Congress of Berlin, Kogălniceanu had hinted broadly at the likelihood of revenge against the Jewish community. Though this did not occur in the form of pogroms, retribution was forthcoming in a more dismal constitutional status (i.e., that of being "apatrid" or stateless) and in the miserly according of citizenship. Even after World War I the Allies would still be badgering the Romanians to observe their obligations under the Treaty of Berlin.[28] In the period from the proclamation of the Kingdom through the first decade of the twentieth century, the labyrinthine, highly politicized naturalization process produced on average approximately 30 Jewish-Romanian nationals a year. On the eve of the First World War, if we discount the some 1,000 veterans emancipated as a gesture of good faith in 1879, only 529 additional Jewish citizens had been added to the rolls as a result of Great Power intervention in the domestic affairs of Romania. Ranging from zero in some years to a high of 52 in 1880 Bucharest meted out equality of rights in such a way as to serve the anti-Semites' vision of the national interest and to prevent any significant social or political impact of the Jewish population. The Romanians won not only their diplomatic fight, but also succeeded in preserving their stance vis-à-vis the Jews virtually unchanged in practical terms. The thesis based on quality allowed them to perform this feat and subsequently put the best possible face on an ethnic antipathy that was now firmly equated with the national ethos.[29]

---

[27] Iancu, *Les Juifs en Roumanie*, 134, 164, 176, & 180; Berkowitz, *La Question des Israélites en Roumanie*, 677 & 702.

[28] Kogălniceanu, *Opere*, V, 179; Ephraim Natanson, "Romanian Governments and the Legal Status of Jews between the Two World Wars," *Romanian Jewish Studies*, 1 (1987), nr. 1: 51–66.

[29] Berkowitz, *La Question des Israélites*, 724–5; Iancu, *Les Juifs en Roumanie*, 186–9.

Conclusion:
The Logic and Rhetoric
of Anti-Semitism

Romanian nationalism with its omnipresent corollary of anti-Semitism exhibited in the period from 1877 to 1914 a marked self-consciousness. These two factors of phenomenal bias against the Jewish people and romantic exaggeration of ethnic cachet combined to develop a singular stress upon national individuality. In turn this complex often expressed itself with the defensiveness characteristic of a vulnerable state seeking to protect itself against more powerful neighbors. Both convinced that they had won the recent diplomatic struggle and chagrined at the affronts experienced in the process, Romanian anti-Semites gave a hard edge to the recently expanded definition of a "true Romanian." Being a staunch citizen now meant to assume all the baggage, historical and cultural, of the nationalist becoming virtually indistinguishable from the crowd.[1] Anti-Semitism became melded to the aggrieved nationalist's sense of being slighted politically and treated condescendingly where his cultural heritage came into question. Endemic in the relationship with their Jews was the Romanians' perception of their dignity as a people and as a state which suffered in the diplomatic crisis of 1877–1880. Future protestations from without the country relative to anti-Jewish disabilities, then, could be fended off in the manner already described as well as addressed as hostile. The Jew in Romania, therefore, would be identified as stateless (*"apatrid"*) and as

---

[1] M. Eminescu, *Opera politică*, I(1870–1879), I. Crețu (ed.), (București: Cugetarea – Georgescu Delafras, 1941), 545–6.

an element associated with unpleasant memories of international intervention.[2]

In the Romania of the late nineteenth and early twentieth centuries the anti-Semitic core of that country's nationalism left no place for the hundreds of thousands of Jews who never managed to obtain citizenship under the supposedly liberalized rules of 1879. As one indigenous critic put it, in a modern state such as this if the individual is not a citizen, then "he does not exist"—certainly he does not exist as a valued or necessarily tolerated participant in the country's life. Consequently, the large, stateless, Jewish populace automatically bore the attentions and animosity of the nationalist.[3] The intelligentsia and other politically aware Romanians, then, demonstrated a marked anti-Semitic mentality even before the Congress of Berlin. With the Congress and the intertwined struggles over independence and naturalization the nationalistic factor assumed paramount importance on the Romanian political scene. The numbers and personal traits of what we have seen delineated as an invading Jewish army came to pose a major threat to the national identity, its continued evolution and even existence, in the estimation of the zealous anti-Semitic intellectual. However he surveyed the impact of this group, that individual decried its endangering the dominant position of the Romanians in their own state. But this threat could be reduced, if the numbers involved were lowered. As ominous as this sounds to the modern ear, it did not necessarily connote unlimited violence though it might portend the brutal pogroms for which Romania reaped well deserved obloquy.[4]

A specifically anti-Jewish xenophobia became endemic among the doctrines of the ardent Romanian nationalist. Politically as well as culturally this antipathy took root in both halves of the ideological spectrum enabling liberal and conservative to garner support with it. Approaching at times the emotional

---

[2] Carol Iancu, *Les Juifs en Roumanie 1866–1919, de l'Exclusion à l'Emancipation* (Aix-en-Provence: Editions de l'Université de Provence, 1978), 176; *Independența României, Documente, IV (Documente Diplomatice, 1873–1881)*, (București: Editura Academiei Republicii Socialiste România, 1978), 343.

[3] Constantin Dobrogeanu-Gherea, "Gherea și chestiunea evreiască [Interviu]," *Opere complete*, V. 5 (București: Editura Politică, 1973), 168.

[4] Mihail Kogălniceanu, *Opere*, V (București: Editura Academiei Republicii Socialiste România, 1984), 167; M. Eminescu, *Opera politică*, II(1880–1883), I. Crețu (ed.), (București: Cugetarea—Georgescu Delafras, 1941), 389.

intensity of an unbridled chauvinism, this anti-Semitic component of Romanian nationalism focused on preserving the
integrity of the country's traditions and ethnicity. The Jewish
issue analyzed from this point of view coincided with a potential derogation of Romania's individuality. Anti-Semitism came
to constitute a fundamental portion of defending the national
interest and uniqueness.[5] Whereas being an anti-Semite in
other countries might evoke reactions associated with sordid
and borderline intellections, it did not constitute an extremist
position in Romania. What adjustment had occurred in the
status of the Jewish community had not come from an amelioration of relations between it and gentile society but instead
as a result of Great Power intimidation. A natural outgrowth
of native nationalism and wounded pride, anti-Semitism took
its place matter of factly as a presupposed element of the
intelligentsia's outlook on life. To be Romanian was to be instinc-
tively anti-Jewish.[6] As a constituent part of the "general con-
sensus" in the Kingdom of Romania from the mid-nineteenth
century on, nationalism with this pronounced ingredient of
ethnic jaundice also generated Romanian assertiveness where
the Jews were concerned. This combative attribute we have
seen in the argumentation and dramatics of the anti-Semitic
intellectuals of the period.[7] Though sometimes consciously
overstated there can be no doubt of both the verbal aggressive-
ness and innate connection between this new nationalism and
its xenophobic, anti-Semitic counterpart. Unfortunately, the
intellectuals who indulged themselves in broadcasting this theoretical bias attempted to draw too fine a line. When popular-
ized and conveyed to the Romanian populace at large, the militant quality of this anti-Jewish theme led to violence despite
repeated disclaimers by the intelligentsia. Certainly the careful

---

[5] Stephen Fischer-Galati, "Romanian Nationalism," *Nationalism in Eastern Europe*,
Peter F. Sugar & Ivo J. Lederer (eds.), (Seattle: University of Washington Press, 1969),
385–6; Paul Lendvai, *Anti-Semitism Without Jews, Communist Eastern Europe* (Garden
City: Doubleday & Co., Inc., 1971), 327.

[6] Nicholas M. Nagy-Talavera, *The Green Shirts and the Others, A History of Fascism
in Hungary and Rumania* (Stanford: Hoover Institution Press, 1970), 348; Ephraim
Natanson, "Romanian Governments and the Legal Status of Jews between the Two
World Wars," *Romanian Jewish Studies*, 1 (1987), nr. 1: 56.

[7] Eugen Weber, "The Men of the Archangel," *International Fascism, 1920–1945*, Walter
Laquer & George L. Mosse (eds.), (New York: Harper Torchbooks, 1966), 104; Henry
L. Roberts, *Rumania: Political Problems of an Agrarian State* (New Haven: Yale University
Press, 1951), 224.

differentiation between requiring baptism of Jews for the secular purpose of interbreeding and the similar demand made
by partisans of traditional religious bigotry proved to be beyond
the ken of many more artless minds.[8]

Even among the intelligentsia, a religious aspect of Romanian nationalism and hence of anti-Semitism had existed for
centuries. As we have seen repeatedly, however, the nation's
politicians and ideologues continually denied a history of religiously motivated discrimination—much less persecution.
Though a shading of the truth, in their own minds they were
accurate in that they did not define the Jewish danger primarily
in sectarian terms. The threat component, so inextricably a
part of the design of both Romanian nationalism and anti-
Semitism, resided far more in the economic presence of the
Jewish community.[9] In Romania Jews stood out as an ever
present irritation in the market and an invariable reminder of
domestic economic difficulties. Though employing the vernacular of stereotypical religious anti-Semitism, since that comprised the extent of peasant understanding and vocabulary,
the propelling motif was more that of economic scrutiny. The
Jew, then, symbolized for the intellectual the alien who victimized the peasant economically, and the peasant represented
for all these men, but especially for the thoroughgoing anti-
Semites from rural Moldavia, the fundamental texture of the
Romanian nation. Iorga even had an idealized representation
of a male and female peasant on the masthead of his news-
paper, *Neamul Romanesc* (*The Romanian People*). While the Jew
might differ in his method of worship, the intelligentsia saw
him more in the mode of a menace to the livelihood of the
nation's backbone, the peasantry.[10] The established tradition
of anti-Semitism by the twentieth century, then, was one of
exploitation of this theme by the intelligentsia and politicians
for their own purposes. The peasantry might explode as it did

---

[8] Șt. Zeletin, *Burghezia română* (București: Cultura Națională, 1925), 230; A. D.
Xenopol, "Patriotizmul," *Arhiva Societății științifice și literare din Iași*, 17 (1906), nr. 7/8:
348–9.

[9] Nagy-Talavera, *The Green Shirts*, 356; Frederick Kellogg, "The Structure of Romanian Nationalism," *Canadian Review of Studies in Nationalism*, 11 (1984), nr. 1: 32.

[10] Fritz Stern, *Gold and Iron. Bismarck, Bleichröder, and the Building of the German
Empire* (New York: Vintage Books, 1979), 354–5; Eugen Weber, "Romania," *The European Right*, Hans Rogger & Eugen Weber (eds.), (Berkeley & Los Angeles: University
of California Press, 1966), 505 & 569.

in 1907, directing much of its anger against the Jews, but this constituted more an economic reaction than a religious one. Other nationalities serving in the same economic roles as the Jews also came in for similar treatment. Jews simply stood out because of their numbers and culture. Lacking marketplace contentiousness as was the norm, Romanian peasant and Jew were more likely to live in quiet and destitute proximity than to bicker. This remained the province of the articulate intellectual as well as that of the activist university student.[11]

Inherent in the anti-Semitic discussion of religion as well as in its other tenets generally we find a pronounced inconsistency. Due to the ad hoc nature of the argumentation, Romanian anti-Semites (and sometimes the same theorist in varying circumstances) often held conflicting positions. On such topics as the usefulness to the nation of the Jewish population, the advisability and potential for assimilation, and the necessity of conversion, the cant fluctuated to fit the then current situation. The vacillations of the Romanian anti-Semite on these and similar points have their explanation in the overriding goal of the bias; namely, to exalt and preserve the pristine ethnic-historical basis of the nation. Where the utility of Jewish citizenship was concerned, the anti-Semite qualified his argument because of the large numbers involved. A few Jews might be helpful, but not the number present in Moldavia. This kind of nationalist rejected any line of reasoning based on vague idealistic conceptualizations of human nature, preferring the practical to the abstract. In the diplomatic attestations of the period under discussion, this inconsistency sometimes gave the appearance of the scholastic's "strict mental reservation," saying one thing for appearances in a given situation and then altering the professed stand to suit another pose. In the nationalist's mind, however, the focus of attention was always the nation, not the Jew. If the relative numbers of Jews and Armenians in Romania had been reversed, the nationalist would theoretically have castigated the latter group in an analogous manner.[12]

---

[11] Ghitta Sternberg, *Stefanesti, Portrait of a Romanian Shtetl* (Oxford: Pergamon Press, 1984), 29–30 & 253.

[12] Dobrogeanu-Gherea, "Gherea și chestiunea evreiască," 169–70; E. Lovinescu, *T. Maiorescu*, II (1876–1917), (București: Fundația pentru Literatură și Artă "Regele Carol II," 1940), 5–1.

This element of inconsistency became evident and most critical for the minority population, when the process of assimilation was debated. No agreement emerged between the extreme of Eminescu on the right and the more moderate position of a Kogălniceanu,[13] but diversity of opinion on the acceptability of Jewish entrance into the nation did manifest itself. No doctrinal stone wall excluding them developed among the intellectual elite. And to be candid, an additional ingredient contributing to the inconsistency, or political wariness, was the liability of being branded a "philosemite." Thus, on occasion Eminescu reversed his seemingly categorical denials of the possibility of Jewish assimilation. Kogălniceanu, who opted for assimilation and the utility argument, protected himself with the use of ethnic epithets and a guardedly stated standpoint.[14] The interplay of ideas, logic, and rhetoric in Romanian anti-Semitism's stance on assimilation best displayed itself in the works of Xenopol. There we discover the delicate status of the Jewish population and the ambivalent attitude, especially regarding overt actions and not merely bombast, of the nationalist. Quite importantly we also learn from him that assimilation required the disappearance of all signs of a distinctive culture. Mixed with irritation at the Jewish community, Xenopol and others exhibited an envy mingled with admiration. The Jew had talents and drive that Romanians lacked and needed. Rather than hate and violence, the practical overture to the Jewish problem consisted in having them baptized as a prelude to intermarriage. In place of the racially conscious exclusivity of the twentieth century, the lore of the nationalist in Romania continued to deemphasize the religious nature of Judaism and stress the acquisition for the nation of the commendable qualities of the Jewish mercantile element.[15] Even this modicum of beneficence involved difficulties. The current of Romanian anti-Semitism, though often exceptionally brutal, did not involve the single-minded fanaticism of a later day which

---

[13] Eminescu, *Opera politică*, I, 472, 480, 539, & 545–6; Kogălniceanu, *Opere*, V, 177; D. Murărașu, *Naționalismul lui Eminescu* (București: Institutul de Arte Grafice "Bucovina" I. E. Torouțiu, 1932), 147–49.

[14] Bogdan Petriceicu Hasdeu, *Scrieri Literare, Morale și Politice*, II, Mircea Eliade (ed.), (București: Fundația pentru Literatură și Artă "Regele Carol II," 1937), 331–2.

[15] A. D. Xenopol, "Patriotizmul," *Arhiva Societății științifice și literare din Iași*, 17 (1906), nr. 7/8; 348–9; A. D. Xenopol, "Naționalism și Antisemitism," *Noua Revistă Română*, 5 (1909), nr. 18: 277.

hunted the Jew for simply being what he was. It did include, however, a component of mutual incomprehension which effectively separated the world of the gentile nationalist from that of the Jewish population. The outstanding Romanian raconteur of the twentieth century, Mihail Sadoveanu (1880–1961), presented in his short story "The School" an atypically sensitive and humane view of this purblindness. Investigating the differences in culture and quality between the Jewish and Romanian worlds, he provided from his countrymen's point of view an insight into the determinative impact of national environment on each successive generation. A well told tale, "The School" offers the outside observer some inkling of the ethnic's wonder at the other world and his inability to cross the chasm dividing him from it. It likewise sums up much of what we have seen in the anti-Semites' sense of the Jew's extraneous character and envious esteem for certain Jewish capacities.[16]

Romanian anti-Semitism represents an extremely mixed bag, then, of hyperbole, indecisions, and considerable force. It differs fundamentally in character and scope, however, from the relentlessly fanatical variety of the modern totalitarian state. Obviously, there simply does not exist a "good anti-Semitism," and no brief is being made to place the Romanian type in such a fictitious category. For the reasons investigated in this study, mostly self-serving in a nationalistic sense, Romanian anti-Semitism did have certain limits. This did not always protect the individual's life and property nor forestall the savagery discussed in the introduction, but as Eminescu tried to elaborate, this peculiar form of bias did embrace an "ethic of nationalism," one allowing for vitriolic expression and conducive to popular animosities leading to pogroms. It did possess a putative positive savor in that it was directed towards Romanian "supremacy" and not per se against the Jews. According to Eminescu, the mission of nationalism consisted in preserving Romanian culture and dominance without engaging in a megalomaniacal aggression.[17] Thus, though violence of the worst sort might occur, the bureaucracy constituted the more usual Romanian mechanism for frustrating Western humanitarian

---

[16] Mihail Sadoveanu, "The School," *Evening Tales* (New York: Twayne Publishers, Inc., 1962), 72–81.

[17] Murăşu, *Naţionalismul lui Eminescu*, 309.

norms and expressing this deeply ingrained anti-Semitism. The list of specifications and bureaucratic procedures drawn up to implement the post-Berlin naturalization process clearly illustrated this approach. Given the paltry number of Jewish naturalizations before World War I, the Romanian anti-Semites successfully repulsed the drive for Jewish citizenship and served their version of the country's vested interests by simply manipulating the required slips of paper.[18]

Maiorescu in his role as littérateur as well as anti-Semite best summed up this combination of endorsement of bias and theoretical forbearance of violence in one of his more curious aphorisms: "The means are superior to the end and regulate its value. Accordingly, the phrase of the Jesuits should be reversed: the means justify the end."[19] While not accrediting the calumny directed against the Society of Jesus, the aphorism does illuminate the basic structure of Romanian anti-Semitism. Prejudice against the Jewish population, though occasionally qualified by an invidious respect, represented a given. No serious discussion of any consequence existed on this level. Regardless of the bravado of anti-Semitic rhetoric, its proclaimed logic prohibited extermination—though it looked equivocally askance at the occasional violence it precipitated in the infamous Romanian pogroms. The Jew in Romania was deemed a necessary inconvenience, if not an evil, who could usually be dealt with adequately by bureaucratic means and political disingenuousness.

In the period after World War I, these attitudes continued to constitute the main thrust of Romanian anti-Semitism. Indeed, the Romanian state found itself combatting many of the same problems that so exercised it when it became an independent nation; namely, further migration of Jews from Galicia and Russia as well as foreign intervention in the legal affairs of the country to enhance the position of the Jewish community. The familiar issues of the magnitude of the influx and the alien culture of the new population arose in a twentieth century context. And, as might be expected, the question of "quality" emerged heightened by the exoticness of the appear-

---

[18] See 86 & 189–90.

[19] "*Mijlocul e superior scopului și-i regulează valoarea. Prin urmare, fraza iezuiților trebuie întoarsă; mijlocul justifică scopul.*" in Titu Maiorescu, *Critice*, II. Domnica Filimon-Stoicescu (ed.), (București: Editura pentru Literatura, 1967), 494.

ance of these new inhabitants of "Greater Romania" with its vastly expanded borders. Especially in the case of Nicolae Iorga these traditional nationalistic and anti-Semitic concepts had a profound impact on the leadership of the Romanian fascist organization, the Iron Guard.[20] Romanian anti-Semitism, then, remained true to its conventions manifesting pre-twentieth century or (if we are thinking in terms of totalitarian regimes) pre-modern characteristics. Dr. Dorian, with his customarily trenchant observations on the nature of Romanian society in the era just before and during World War II, described the mentality of the intelligentsia as exhibited in the person of the preeminent literary critic Eugen Lovinescu (1882–1948). As in the epoch after independence, such members of the elite could conduct themselves in a quite civilized fashion (to employ a favorite Romanian distinction) while at the same time "coldly, amicably" declaring their anti-Semitic views.[21] The founder of the Iron Guard, Corneliu Zelea Codreanu (1899–1938), and the other leaders of his fascist movement likewise had their roots in this traditional anti-Jewish prejudice with its nationalistic-xenophobic emphasis. Their fundamental ideas exposed the same base orientation as their less radical fellow anti-Semites. They, however, did not stop at verbal demonstrations of their virulent attitudes. Though sharing the same core concepts, they did not draw the fine line between the traditionally blatant anti-Semitism and a thoroughgoing physical expression of their bias. And in this they developed an extremist and atypical manifestation of Romanian prejudice.[22]

The fate of Romania's Jews and their fortuitously providential survival during the obscenity of the Final Solution resulted rather from the fact that Marshal Antonescu embodied the main traits of his country's anti-Semitism without the racial element

---

[20] Emil Dorian, *The Quality of Witness, A Romanian Diary 1937–1944*, trans. Mara Soceanu Vamos (Philadelphia: The Jewish Publication Society of America, 1982), xxiv, xxvii–xxviii, & 108; Teodor Armon, "'Enemies' and 'Traitors'–Aspects of the Antisemitism of the Iron Guard," *Romanian Jewish Studies*, 1 (1987), nr. 1: 68.

[21] Dorian, *The Quality of Witness*, 114.

[22] Carol Iancu, *Les Juifs en Roumanie (1866–1919), de l'Exclusion à l'Emancipation* (Aix-en-Provence: Editions de l'Université de Provence, 1978), p. 134; Eugen Weber, "The Men of the Archangel," *International Fascism, 1920–1945*, Walter Laqueur & George L. Mosse (eds.), (New York: Harper Torchbooks, 1966), 107; Eugen Weber, "Romania," *The European Right*, Hans Rogger & Eugen Weber (eds.), (Berkeley & Los Angeles: University of California Press, 1966), 570.

of the totalitarian fanatic. In contrast to the Iron Guard members and the Germans, his concern focused on the well being of Romania and the fortunes of war, not primarily on the Jews. He, like the nineteenth century politicians and intellectuals we have discussed, distinguished between types of Jews: those who belonged to Romania proper (the "Old Kingdom" with its pre-World War I frontiers) and those who were alien or enemies.[23] And like those earlier leaders Antonescu sought to pursue a unique Jewish policy and his definition of the nation's self-interest by balancing between Great Power demands. As Prince Carol had complained in his own instance, the *Conducătorul* found himself trying to offset the nationalistic anxieties of his country against both domestic and foreign pressures. And like the intelligentsia of the period before the First World War Antonescu too had to think in terms of the usefulness of Romania's Jews, or in the jargon of the twentieth century in terms of the "cost-and-benefits" ratio of various Jewish policies. This complex of traditional Romanian anti-Semitism and the exigencies of modern warfare allowed for horrendous atrocities, for a mixture of casual brutality and venality, but did not permit methodically wholehearted participation in the Final Solution.[24] Even when the Iron Guard was concerned, with its more modern and racially oriented ideas, the anti-Jewish violence focused primarily along traditional lines; namely, against the Jews outside the Old Kingdom and against those seen as distinctly different from the assimilated community of Moldavia and Wallachia. For a variety of reasons, Marshal Antonescu warily kept the Nazis at bay and refused to cooperate fully in their anti-Jewish measures. Whatever the self-serving and defensive nature of this caution may have been, it also included in one commentator's words an "ideological gap between Romanian and Nazi anti-Semitism." Despite the violence, inconsistency, and inanity of Antonescu's Jewish policies as well as the barbarism of the Iron Guard pogroms, the Nazis saw the Romanians as being pro-Jewish. That "ideological gap" meant that Romanian policies regarding the Jews con-

---

[23] Dorian, *The Quality of Witness*, xxx; Jean Ancel, "The Jassy Syndrome (I)," *Romanian Jewish Studies*, 1 (1987), nr. 1: 42.

[24] *Aus dem Leben König Karls von Rumänien; Aufzeichnungen eines Augenzeugen*, IV (Stuttgart: Cotta'sche Buchhandlung, 1900), 225; Dorian, *The Quality of Witness*, xxx & 228.

tinued along the track prescribed by the country's customary anti-Semitism, not the more thoroughgoing Nazi type.[25] As we would expect given the development of Romanian anti-Semitism in the nineteenth and early twentieth centuries, Antonescu's Jewish policies during World War II largely flowed from tactical and self-interested considerations related to Romanian nationalistic values. They reflected neither high ethical concerns nor the spite of the convinced fascist. Rather like the politicians and intellectuals quoted earlier in this study Antonescu employed the Jewish question as he perceived it to be useful for the nation. After 1942 the only sweeping plan he considered for the elimination of Jews from Romanian soil centered on the export of some tens of thousands to the Middle East (at a considerable price per head, of course). To the very end of the war, the Romanian government refused to participate in what the Nazis wanted in the way of a complete solution to the Jewish question. Indeed, as was mentioned in the "Introduction," beginning in the spring of 1944 with the mass deportations of Hungarian Jews to the extermination camps, the Romanians cooperated to some slight degree in efforts to smuggle them into the southern half of Transylvania.[26] Perhaps uncomfortably for those of a tidy mind, Romanian anti-Semitism in World War II, consistent with its foundations, demonstrated neither humanitarian characteristics nor doctrinaire tendencies. As Dr. Dorian stressed, for the Jews living in the Old Kingdom the cardinal point—indeed the only one that mattered ultimately—was that whatever the Romanian motivations the anti-Semitic policies desired by the Nazis and implemented in other areas were not systematically enforced there.

Returning, then, to Hannah Arendt's observations that, "It is hardly an exaggeration to say that Rumania was the most anti-Semitic country in prewar Europe," and ". . . even the S.S. were taken aback, and occasionally frightened, by the horrors of old-fashioned, spontaneous pogroms on a gigantic scale . . . ," we must note that she is correct to a degree.[27] The anti-

---

[25] Andreas Hillgruber, "Anhang I. Die Judenfrage als Problem der Deutsch-Rumänischen Beziehungen," *Hitler, König Carol und Marschall Antonescu, Die Deutsch-Rumänischen Beziehungen 1938–1944* (Wiesbaden: Franz Steiner Verlag, 1965), 237 & 239–41; Dorian, *The Quality of Witness*, xxxii.

[26] Hillgruber, *Hitler, König Carol und Marschall Antonescu*, 241–6; Dorian, *The Quality of Witness*, 246 & 270.

[27] Hannah Arendt, *Eichmann in Jerusalem* (New York: Viking Press, 1963), 172.

Semitism here, however, does not correspond to that of the Nazis. Summed up in the aphorism of Maiorescu was the idea of limits to prejudice, of enlightened self-interest, and even of the humanity of the Jew (though qualitatively different from that of the Romanians). The shock value of violently expressed Romanian anti-Semitism, of the pogroms, consisted in the lack of style and the grossness of the brutality. We find here none of the cool efficiency and order of a Germanic enterprise. But once again in Dr. Dorian's words it is ". . . simply ridiculous if you become selective about the shades of brutality that are to arouse your indignation."[28] Romanian savagery towards the "alien" or "enemy" Jew was all too real, and in contrast to an Eichmann, they did not proclaim that they were not anti-Semites. They were, and they specifically embraced that bias as an integral part of their nationalism. Using Elie Wiesel's distinction regarding the dehumanizing of the Jewish population by the Nazis, however, Romanian anti-Semitism did not render the Jew simply an object to be destroyed. In the Old Kingdom, at least, the Jew remained human—although abused in a horrific and criminal manner that epitomized man's inhumanity to man,[29] he was not merely written off as a disposable, inert commodity. Viewing the Jewish population in this fashion permitted both the barbarities with all the deficiency of methodology deplored by the Nazis and likewise the final survival of a majority of the Jewish population in the Old Kingdom. Instead of being a number, the Romanian Jew continued in the eyes of the nationalistic anti-Semite to be a disliked human being for whom occasionally there might be a use advantageous to the nation. The fortuitous fact of being a Jew in Romania, therefore, made all the difference for some 400,000 members of the European Jewish community. Though brutal and intellectually shallow, Romanian anti-Semitism was providential for them in that its vagaries and divergence from the modern norm allowed them to survive.

---

[28] Dorian, *The Quality of Witness*, 197.
[29] Elie Wiesel, "An Appointment with Hate," *Commentary*, 34 (1962), nr. 6: 476.

Bibliography

A. PRIMARY SOURCES

Aus dem Leben König Karls von Rumanien; Aufzeichnungen eines Augenzeugen, Vols. I–IV. Stuttgart: Cotta'sche Buchhandlung, 1894–1900.

Breviarul statistic al Republicii Socialiste România, 1966. Bucureşti: Direcţia Centrală de Statistică, 1966.

British and Foreign State Papers, "Correspondence between Great Britain and Turkey Respecting the Persecution of Jews in Moldavia," Vol. LVIII (1867–1868).

British and Foreign State Papers, "Correspondence relative to the Recognition of the Independence of Romania – 1879–1880," Vol. LXXI (1879–1880).

British and Foreign State Papers, "Roumanian Declaration of Independence," Vol. LXVIII (1876–1877).

Corespondenţa Generalului Iancu Ghica 2 Aprilie 1877-8 Aprilie 1878. General Radu R. Rosetti (ed.). Bucureşti: "Cartea Românească," 1930.

Documente privind Istoria României, Războiul pentru Independenţă, Vols. I–IX. Bucureşti: Editura Academiei Republicii Populare Române, 1952–1955.

Documents diplomatiques français (1871–1914), Vs. 2 & 3. 1re série. Paris: Imprimerie Nationale, 1930-31.

Independenţa României, Documente, Vols. I–IV. Bucureşti: Editura Academiei Republicii Socialiste România, 1977-78.

Nouveau recueil général de Traités, et autres actes relatifs aux rapports de droit international. Continuation du grand recueil de G. Fr. de Martens. Vols. III(1878) & VIII(1833). 2nd. ser. Göttingen: Librairie de Dieterich.

B. SECONDARY SOURCES

Adăniloaie, Nichita. "Berlin," *Reprezentanţele Diplomatice ale României,* Vol. I (1859–1917). Bucureşti: Editura Politică, 1967.

Ancel, Jean. "The Jassy Syndrome (I)," *Romanian Jewish Studies,* I (1987), nr. 1: 33-49.

———. "The Jassy Syndrome (II)," *Romanian Jewish Studies,* I (1987), nr. 2: 35-52.

Anderson, M. S. *The Eastern Question, 1774-1923.* New York: St. Martin's Press, 1966.

Anghelescu, Gh. F. & Gh. Buzatu. "Din arhiva istorică a României contemporane (III): generalul Titus Gârbea despre ultima întrevedere Hitler-Antonescu," *Anuarul Institutul de Istorie și Arheologie "A. D. Xenopol,"* XXIII (1986), 815–20.

"A Policy Respectful of Minorities," *Romania Today,* 1985, nr. 6: 21.

Arendt, Hannah. *Eichmann in Jerusalem.* New York: Viking Press, 1963.

Armon, Teodor. "'Enemies' and 'Traitors'–Aspects of the Antisemitism of the Iron Guard," *Romanian Jewish Studies,* I (1987), nr. 1: 67–76.

Bagdasar, N. *Istoria Filosofiei Românești.* Ediția a II-a. București: Societatea Română de Filosofie, 1941.

Barbolov, Gheorghi. "Politica balcanică a României in anii 1875–1877," *Revista de Istorie,* 40 (1987), nr. 4: 397–407.

Bărbulescu, Petre (ed.). *Reprezentanțele diplomatice ale României,* Vol. I. București: Editura Politică, 1967.

Berceanu, Barbu B. "Modificarea, din 1879, a articolului 7 din Constituție," *Studii și materiale de istorie modernă,* VI (1979): 67–89.

Berindei, Dan. *Independent Romania, 1877.* Trans. Leon Levitcni. Bucharest: Meridiane Publishing House, 1976.

Berkowitz, Joseph. *La Question de Israélites en Roumanie.* Paris: Jouve et Cie, 1923.

Bodunescu, Ion. *Diplomația românească în slujba independenței.* Iași: Editura Junimea, 1978.

Boicu, L. & Al. Zub (eds.). *A. D. Xenopol, Studii privitoare la viața și opera sa.* București: Editura Republicii Socialiste România, 1972.

Bossy, Raoul, V. *Politica externă a României între anii 1873–1880 privită deal Agenția diplomatică din Roma.* București: Cultura Națională, 1928.

Botez, Octav. *Alexandru Xenopol, Teoretician și Filosof al Istoriei.* București: Tipografia Ion C. Vacărescu, 1928.

Braham, Randolph L. "The Uniqueness of the Holocaust in Hungary," in *The Holocaust in Hungary Forty Years Later,* Randolph L. Braham & Bela Vago (eds.). New York: Social Science Monographs, Columbia University Press, 1985, 177–190.

Brătianu, George I. *La politique extérieure du Roi Charles I-er de Roumanie.* București: "Cartea Românescă," 1940.

———. *Origines et formation de l'unité roumanie.* Bucarest: Institute d'Histoire Universelle "N. Iorga," 1943.

Burks, Richard V. "Romania and the Balkan Crisis of 1875–78," *Journal of Central European Affairs,* 2 (1942): 119–134 & 3 (1942): 310–320.

Călinescu, G. *Istoria Literaturii Române.* București: Fundatia Regală pentru Literatură și Artă, 1941.

Carp, Matatias. *Cartea Neagra, Suferințele Evreilor din România 1940–1944.* I–III. Bucharest, 1946–48.

Cazan, Gh. "Recunoașterea internațională a independenței de stat a României," *Reprezentanțele Diplomatice ale României,* Vol. I (1859–1917). București: Editura Politică, 1967.

Căzănișteanu, Constantin & Mihail E. Ionescu. *Războiul neatîrnării Romaniei, 1877–1878.* București: Editura Știintifică și Enciclopedică, 1977.

Căzănișteanu, Constantin. "The 1877–1878 War for the Conquest of Romania's

State Independence," *Nouvelles Études d'Histoire*. Bucureşti: Editura Academiei Republicii Academiei Socialiste România, 1975), 159–173.

Chiriţă, Gr. "Attitudes puterilor europene faţă de proclamarea independenţei României," *Revista de Istorie*, 30 (1977), 4:673–690.

Ciachir, Nicolae. *Războiul pentru independenţa României în contextul European (1875–1878)*. Bucureşti: Editura Ştiinţifică şi Enciclopedică, 1977.

Constantinescu, Miron et al. *Istoria României*. Bucureşti: Editura Didactică şi Pedagogică, 1969.

Corivan, N. *Lupta diplomatică pentru cucerirea independenţei României*. Bucureşti: Editura Ştiinţifică şi Enciclopedică, 1970.

———. "Proclamarea independenţei României şi atitudinea marilor puteri," *Cercetari istorice*. Iaşi: Muzeul de Istorie a Moldovei, 1977, 325–43.

———. *Relaţiile diplomatice ale României de la 1859 la 1877*. Bucureşti: Editura Ştiinţifică şi Enciclopedică, 1984.

Damé, Frédéric. *Histoire de la Roumanie Contemporaine*. Paris: Germer Baillière et Cie, 1900.

Dinu, Marcel, Octavian Gaurisi, & Cornel Paraschiv. "Dezvoltarea relaţiilor internaţionale ale României," *Diplomaţia Română în slujba independenţei*. Bucureşti: Editura Politică, 1977, 238–68.

Dobrogeanu-Gherea, Constantin. "Gherea şi chestiunea evreiască [Interviu]," *Opere compete*. v. 5. Bucureşti: Editura Politică, 1973, 168–71.

Dorian, Emil. *The Quality of Witness, A Romanian Diary 1937–1944*. Trans. Mara Soceanu Vamos. Philadelphia: The Jewish Publication Society of America, 1982.

Dragan, Mihai. *B. P. Hasdeu*. Iaşi: Editura Junimea, 1972.

Dumitrescu-Buşulenga, Zoe. "Eminescu, A National and World Poet," *Romania Today*, 1988, nr. 6: 42–3.

Edwards, H. Sutherland. *Sir William White*. London: John Murray, 1902.

Eminescu, M. *Opera politică*. I (1870–79) & II (1880–83), I. Creţu (ed.). Bucureşti: Cugetarea–Georgescu Delafras, 1941.

Fătu, Mihai & Ion Spălăţelu. *Garda de Fier, organizaţie teroristă de tip fascist*. Bucureşti: Editura Politică, 1971.

——— & Mircea Musat (eds.). *Horthyist-Fascist Terror in Northwestern Romania, September 1940–October 1944*, Bucharest: Meridiane Publishing House, 1985.

Fischer-Galati, Stephen. "Romanian Nationalism," in *Nationalism in Eastern Europe*, Peter F. Sugar & Ivo J. Lederer (eds.). Seattle: University of Washington Press, 1969, 373–395.

Gane, C. P. *P. Carp, şi locul sau in istoria politică a ţării*, V. I. Bucureşti: Editura Ziarului "Universul," 1936.

Giurescu, Constantin C. *Viaţa şi opera lui Cuza Vodă*. Bucureşti: Editura Ştiinţifică, 1966.

Gliga, V. et al. *Diplomaţia română în slujba independenţei*. Bucureşti: Editura Politică, 1977.

Gogoneaţă, N. & Z. Ornea. *A. D. Xenopol, concepţia socială şi filozofică*. Bucureşti: Editura Ştiinţifică, 1965.

Hasdeu, B. P. *Istoria Critica a Romaniloru*. V. II. Bucuresci: Typographia Antoniu Manescu, 1874.

————. *Sic Cogito*. București: Editura Librariei "Univerala" Alcalay & Co., n.d.

Hilburg, Raul. *The Destruction of the European Jews*. Chicago: Quadrangle Books, 1961.

Hillgruber, Andreas. "Anhang I. Die Judenfrage als Problem der deutsch-rumänischen Beziehungen," in *Hitler, König Carol und Marschall Antonescu, die Deutsch-Rumänischen Beziehungen, 1938–1944*. Wiesbaden: Franz Steiner Verlag, 1965.

Iancu, Carol. *Les Juifs en Roumaine (1866–1919), de l'Exclusion à l'Emancipation*. Aix-en-Provence: Editions de l'Université de Provence, 1978.

Ibrăileanu, G. *Mihai Eminescu, studii și articole*. Iași: Editura Junimea, 1974.

Ionașcu, Ion, Petre Bărbulescu, & Gheorghe Gheorghe. *Tratatele internaționale ale României, 1354–1920*. București: Editura Științifică și Enciclopedică, 1975.

Iorga, N. *Correspondance diplomatique roumaine sous le roi Charles Ier (1866–1880)*. Deuxième édition. Bucarest: Bibliothèque de l'Institut pour l'étude de l'Histoire Universelle, 1938.

————. *Histoire des relations russo-roumaines*. Jassy: Édition du journal "Neamul Românesc," 1917.

————. "În chestia evreiască," *Neamul Românesc*, IV, nr. 88: 1401–2; 9 August 1909.

————. "In Chestia Evreiasca, I De Ce Emigrează Evreii?" *Epoca*, VIII, nr. 2034–213: 1; 9 August 1902.

————. "In Chestia Evreiasca, III Doctrina de apărare economică," *Epoca*, VIII, nr. 2077–175: 1; 2 July 1902.

————. "In Chestia Evreiasca, IV Tipurile evreești: proletarul," *Epoca*, VIII, nr. 2087–185: 1; 12 July 1902.

————. *Politica externă a Regelui Carol I*. București: Institutul de Arte Grafice Luceafărul S.A., 1923.

————. "Răscoale terănești," *Neamul Românesc*, I, nr. 86: 522, 4 March 1907.

————. *Războiul pentru independența României*. București: Cultura Națională, 1927.

————. "Romîni și străini," *Neamul Românesc*, I, nr. 93: 629, 25 March 1907.

————. "Sentiment național și ideie națională," *Neamul Românesc*, IV(1909), nr. 147–8: 2493–5.

————. "Sîntem noi șoviniști?" *Neamul Românesc*, I (1906), nr. 66: 193–5.

————. Speech to Adunarea Deputaților in *Desbaterile Adunării Deputaților*. nr. 45: 591–98; 13 February 1910.

Irimia, D. (ed.). *Mihai Eminescu, despre cultură și artă*. Iași: Junimea, 1970.

Istoria Romîniei, IV(1848–1878). P. Constantinescu-Iași (ed.). București: Editura Academiei Republicii Populare Romîne, 1964.

Jelavich, Barbara. "Diplomatic Problems of an Autonomous State: Romanian Decisions on War and Independence, 1877," *Southeastern Europe*, 5 (1978), nr. 1: 26–35.

————. *History of the Balkans*, Vol. I (*Eighteenth and Nineteenth Centuries*). Cambridge: Cambridge University Press, 1983.

————. "Russia and the Reacquisition of Southern Bessarabia 1875–1878," *Südost-Forschungen*, 28 (1969): 199–237.

Jensen, John & Gerhard Rosegger. "Xenophobia or Nationalism? The

Demands of the Romanian Engineering Profession for Preference in Government Contracts, 1898–1905," *East European Quarterly*, 19 (1985), nr. 1: 1–14.

Kanner, Bénédict. *La Société Littéraire Junimea de Iassy et son Influence sur le Mouvement Intellectuel en Roumanie*. Paris: Bonvalot-Jouve, 1906.

Karețki, Aurel & Maria Covaci. *Zile însângerate la Iași*. București: Editura Politică, 1978.

Kellog, Frederick. "The Historiography of Romanian Independence," *East European Quarterly*, XII (1978), 3: 369–377.

————. "The Structure of Romanian Nationalism," *Canadian Review of Studies in Nationalism*, XI (1984), nr. 1: 21–50.

Kogălniceanu, Mihail. "Despre drepturile politice ale străinilor, ale pământenilor de orice religie creștina," *Cuvânt introductiv la cursul de istorie națională și câteva din discursurile in Divanul Ad-Hoc Moldovei*. București: Librăriei Leon Alcalay, 1909, 62–94.

————. "Pentru toleranța religioasa," *Cuvânt introductiv la cursul de istorie națională și câteva din discursurile in Divanul Ad-Hoc Moldovei*. București: Librăriei Leon Alcalay, 1909, 49–58.

————. *Opere*. Vols. I–V. Georgeta Penelea (ed.). București: Academiei Republicii Socialiste România, 1974–1984.

Kohler, Max J. & Simon Wolf. *Jewish Disabilities in the Balkan States*. New York: The American Jewish Committee, 1916.

Kremnitz, Mite. *Regele Carol I al României*. Trans. Const. Graur. București: Editura "Universala" Alcalay & Co., 1909.

Lendvai, Paul. *Anti-Semitism Without Jews, Communist Eastern Europe*. Garden City: Doubleday & Co., Inc., 1971.

Loeb, Isidore. *La Situation des Israélites en Turquie, en Serbie et en Roumanie*. Paris: Joseph Baer et Cie, 1877.

Lovinescu, E. T. *Maiorescu*. I (1840–1876) & II (1876–1917). București: Fundația pentru Literatură și Artă "Regele Carol II," 1940.

Maier, Lothar. "Die Politik Rumäniens in der Orientalischen Krise 1875–1878 aus der Sicht der diplomatischen Vertreter Grossbritanniens und Frankreichs in Bukarest," *Südost-Forschungen*, 40 (1981): 81–103.

Maiorescu, Titu. *Critice*. II. Domnica Filimon-Stoicescu (ed.). București: Editura pentru Literatură, 1967.

————. *Discursuri parlamentare*. I (1866–1876) & II (1876–1881). București: Editura Librăriei Socecŭ & Comp., 1897.

————. *Istoria Contimporană a României (1866–1900)*. București: Editura Librăriei București: Socecŭ & Co., 1925.

Marcu, Alexandru. "Cavour și unirea Principatelor (1856–1859)" in *Omagiul Ramiro Ortiz*. București: n.p., 1930.

Marian, L. *Bogdan Petriceicu Hasdeu*. București: "Cartea Româneasca," 1928.

Maries, Stela. *Supușii străini din Moldova in perioada 1781–1862*. Iași: Universitatea "Al. I. Cuza," 1985.

Marriott, J. A. R. *The Eastern Question*. 4th ed. Oxford: Clarendon Press, 1963.

Medlicott, W. B. "The Recognition of Roumanian Independence, 1878–1880," *Slavonic Review*, 11 (1933), 32: 354–372 & 33: 572–589.

Mehedinți, S. *Din Viața lui Maiorescu*. Extras din Revista *Convorbiri Literare* (Nr. 1/1941). București: I. E. Torouțiu.

Murărașu, D. *Naționalismul lui Eminescu*. București: Institutul de Arte Grafice "Bucovina" I. E. Torouțiu, 1932.

Nagy-Talavera, Nicholas M. *The Green Shirts and the Others, A History of Fascism in Hungary and Rumania*. Stanford: Hoover Institution Press, 1970.

Natanson, Ephraim. "Romanian Governments and the Legal Status of Jews between the Two World Wars," *Romanian Jewish Studies*, 1 (1987), nr. 1: 51–66.

Negruți, Ecaterina. "Situația demografică a Moldovei in secolul al XIX-lea," *Revista de Istorie*, 34 (1981), 2: 243–257.

Oldson, William O. "Nicolae Iorga: The Romanian Nationalist as Historian," *East European Quarterly*, 6 (1973): 473–486.

————. *The Historical and Nationalistic Thought of Nicolae Iorga*. Boulder & New York: East European Monographs, Columbia University Press, 1973.

Ornea, Z. *Junimismul*. București: Editura pentru Literatură, 1966.

Păcurariu, Mircea. *Istoria Bisericii Ortodoxe Române*. V. 3. București: Editura Institutului Biblic si de Misiune al Bisericii Ortodoxe Române, 1981.

Pantazi, Radu (ed.). *C. A. Rosetti, Gînditorul, Omul*. București: Editura Politică, 1969.

Panu, G. *Amintiri dela Junimea din Iași*. I & II. București: Editură "Remus Cioflec," 1905.

Pascu, Ștefan et al. *The Independence of Romania, Selected Bibliography*. București: Editura Academiei Republicii Socialiste România, 1980.

Platon, Gheorghe. "Afirmarea suveranității României în preajma războiului din 1877–1878. Mărturii din arhivele Belgiei," *Studii și Materiale de Istorie Modernă*. Vol. V. București: Editura Academiei Republicii Socialiste România, 1975.

Predescu, Lucian. *Enciclopedia cugetarea*. București: Georgescu Delafras, 1940.

Rădulescu-Zoner, Șerban. "Poziția internațională a României dupa Congresul de la Berlin. Premise de unei opțiuni," *Studii și materiale de Istorie Modernă*. 6(1979): 39–65.

Roberts, Henry L. *Rumania: Political Problems of an Agrarian State*. New Haven: Yale University Press, 1951.

Roth, Cecil. *The History of the Jews of Italy*. Philadelphia: The Jewish Publication Society of America, 1946.

Sadoveanu, Mihail. "The School" in *Evening Tales*. New York: Twayne Publishers, Inc., 1962.

Seton-Watson, R. W. *A History of the Roumanians*. Hamden: Archon Books, 1963.

Simion, A. "The Horthyst Regime of Occupation in North-Western Romania. The Policy vis-à-vis the Non-Maghyar Populations," *Anuarul Institutul de Istorie și Arheologie "A. D. Xenopol,"* 23 (1986): 55–73.

Siupiur, Elena. "The Training of Intellectuals in South-East Europe during the 19th Century. The Romanian Model," *Anuarul Institutul de Istorie și Arheologie "A. D. Xenopol,"* 23 (1986): 469–90.

Southeastern Europe. 5(1978), nr. 1. Special issue: "The Centenary of Romanian Independence, 1878–1978."

Sozan, Michael. "The Jews of Aba," *Eastern European Quarterly*, 20 (1986), nr. 4: 179–97.

Stan, Apostol. *Grupari și curente politice în România între Unire și Independență (1859–1877)*. București: Editura Științifică, 1979.

Stavrianos, L. S. *The Balkans Since 1453*. New York: Holt, Rinehart & Winston, 1965.

Ștefănescu, Marin. *Filosofia Românească*. București: Institutul de Arte Grafice "Răsăritul," 1922.

Ștefănescu, Ștefan et al. *Enciclopedia istoriografiei Românești*. București: Editura Științifică și Enciclopedică, 1978.

Stern, Fritz. *Gold and Iron. Bismarck, Bleichröder, and the Building of the German Empire*. New York: Vintage Books, 1979.

Sternberg, Ghitta. *Stefanesti, Portrait of a Romanian Shtetl*. Oxford: Pergamon Press, 1984.

The Army and The Romanian Society, Al Gh. Savu (ed.). Bucharest: Military Publishing House, 1980.

Theodorescu, Barbu. *Bibliografia istorică și literară a lui N. Iorga*. I (1935) & II (1937). București: Editura "Cartea Românească."

———. *Nicolae Iorga, biobibliografie*. București: Editura Științifică și Enciclopedică, 1976.

Toma, Gheorghe. *Xenopol despre logica istoriei*. București: Editura Politică, 1971.

Torouțiu, I. E. *Studii și Documente Literare*, I–VI. București: Institutul de Arte Grafice "Bucovina," 1931–38.

Vago, Bela. "Contrasting Jewish Leadership in Wartime Hungary and Romania," in *The Holocaust as Historical Experience*. Yehuda Bauer & Nathan Rotenstreich (eds.). New York: Holmes & Meier Publishers, Inc., 1981.

———. *The Shadow of the Swastika, The Rise of Fascism and Anti-Semitism in the Danube Basin*. London: Institute for Jewish Affairs, 1975.

Verax [Radu Rosetti]. *La Roumanie et les Juifs*. Bucarest: I. V. Socecu, 1903.

Weber, Eugen. "Romania," *The European Right*. Hans Rogger & Eugen Weber (eds.). Berkeley: University of California Press, 1966.

———. "The Men of the Archangel," *International Fascism, 1920–1945*. Walter Laqueur & George L. Mosse (eds.). New York: Harper Torchbooks, 1966.

Wiesel, Elie. "An Appointment with Hate," *Commentary*, V. 34 (1962), nr. 6: 470–76.

Winckler, Martin. "Bismarcks Rumänienpolitic und die Durchführung des Artikels 44 des Berliner Vertrages (1878–1880)." Ph.D. dissertation, Ludwig-Maximilians-Universität zu München, 1951.

Xenopol, A. D. "Cultura Națională," *Convorbiri literare*, II (1868), 10:159–63, 11: 181–4, 12: 194–200, 13: 210–15, 14: 231–36, 15: 247–50, 16: 261–5, 17: 280–83.

———. "Curentul Naționalist," *Reînvierea*, I (1903), 1:1–8.

———. "Cuvěntarea festivă rostită la serbarea națională pe mormentul lui Stefan celu Mare," *Convorbiri literare*, V (1871), 12:186–92.

———. *Istoria partidelor politice în România*. I. București: Albert Baer, 1910.

———. "Istoriile Civilisațiunii," *Convorbiri literare*, 3 (1869), 7: 105–9, 8: 121–5, 9: 145–50, 10: 164–70, 12: 203–8, 13: 217–24, 14: 235–40, 15: 251–65, 16: 281–6, 17: 293–301, 18: 309–21.

———. *La Théorie de L'Histoire*. Paris: Ernest Leroux, 1908.

———. "Le Caractere Scientifique de l'Histoire," *Bulletin bibliographique et pedagogique du Mussee belge*, 1914, 223–30.

———. "Lecţiunea de deschidere a cursului de Istoria Românilor de la Universitatea de Iaşi," *Convorbiri literare*, 17 (1883), 8: 300–6.

———. *Les Roumains, Histoire état Matériel et Intellectuel.* Paris: Librairie Ch. Delagrave, 1908.

———. "Nationalism şi Antisemitism," *Noua Revistă Română*, 5 (1909), nr. 18: 276–78.

———. "Naţionalismul," *Noua Revistă Română*, 5 (1908), nr. 3: 36–8.

———. "Opul lui Edgar Quinet 'La création'," *Convorbiri literare*, 5 (1870), nrs. 11: 177–83, 12: 195–99, 13: 206–11, 14: 223–33.

———. "Patriotizmul," *Arhiva Societăţii ştiinţifice şi literare din Iaşi*, 17 (1906), nrs. 7/8: 344–49.

———. "Politique de Races. Roma: Forani E. C. Tip. del Senato, 1903.

———. "Studii asupra stărei noaster actuale," *Convorbiri literare*, 4 (1870), 1: 1–9, 8: 121–31; 5 (1871), 8: 117–28, 15: 233–9, 18: 285–91, 19: 316–23; 11 (1877), 1: 7–17, 2: 41–51; 3: 102–13, 4: 117–24.

Zach, Krista. "Rümaniens kleine Minderheitengruppen nach 1945," *Europa Ethnica*, 39 (1982), nr. 2: 49–62.

Zeletin, Şt. *Burghezia Română, origina şi rolul ei istoric.* Bucureşti: Cultura Naţională, 1925.

Zinger, Zvi. "State of Israel (1948–72)," in *Immigration and Settlement.* Jerusalem: Keter Books, 1973.

Zub, Al. "A. D. Xenopol and the New 'Serial History'," *Revue Roumaine d'Histoire*, 19 (1980), 2/3: 511–19.

———. *A. D. Xenopol, biobibliografie.* Bucureşti: Editura Enciclopedică Română, 1973.

———. *Kogălniceanu, istoric.* Iaşi: Editura Junimea.

Index